PLAY DRUMS NOW 2.5: PLAYING WITH SONGS

~ IDEAL SONG TRAINING ~

- **Skill Level:** LEVEL 2
(prerequisite: 'Play Drums Now 1.0: DRUMSET SKILL BASICS')
(highly recommended: Play Drums Now books 2.1, 2.2, 2.3, 2.4)

- **Estimated Time To Master This Book:**
1-2 months (with regular practice)

- **Goals / Expected Results:**
Well-rounded training in adding drum parts to songs, and increased listening abilities plus song awareness.

- **Next Steps After Completing This Book:**
COMPLETE LEVEL 2 training, with these books:

  - "PLAY DRUMS NOW 2.1: SPORT / RUDIMENTS"
  - "PLAY DRUMS NOW 2.2: RHYTHMS + TIMING"
  - "PLAY DRUMS NOW 2.3: DRUMSET GROOVES"
  - "PLAY DRUMS NOW 2.4: FILLS + DRUM LOOPS"
  - **"PLAY DRUMS NOW 2.5: PLAYING WITH SONGS"** ✓

THEN... PROCEED TO LEVEL 3 MATERIALS!

TABLE OF CONTENTS

- SONGS INFO AND TIPS - p.4

~ **SONG EXERCISES** ~

- (INSTRUCTIONS) - p.12
- **PART I: 16TH NOTE FEEL** - p.13
- (EXERCISE EXAMPLE) - p.14
- **PART II: SWUNG 16TH FEEL** - p.29
- **PART III: 8TH TRIPLET FEEL** - p.35
- **PART IV: 6/8 TIME FEEL** - p.45

- OUTRO / NEXT STEPS - p.49

© 2021 by Adam Randall

All rights reserved. No part of this publication may be reproduced in any form without written permission of the publisher.

ISBN: 9780984436590

www.playdrumsnow.com

THIS BOOK WAS DESIGNED TO BE **THE BEST POSSIBLE TRAINING** FOR ITS PURPOSE, WITH **CAREFULLY CHOSEN** EXERCISES AND INFORMATION.

USED PROPERLY, **THIS BOOK WILL FUNDAMENTALLY ENHANCE YOUR PLAYING.**

~

PLEASE ENJOY THIS BOOK!
-ADAM RANDALL

INSTRUCTIONS FOR THIS BOOK

1) Do your best!

2) Read all the instructions carefully.

3) STAY IN CONTROL (avoid mistakes).

4) Prioritize sound quality.

5) Practice with focus, like you're training for a SPORT.

6) Rehearse patterns thoroughly, like you're memorizing a LANGUAGE.

7) Go generally in order from beginning to end in this book.

8) USE www.PlayDrumsNow.com for more resources.

PLAY DRUMS NOW
THE ULTIMATE DRUMSET TRAINING PROGRAM

USE PROPER TECHNIQUE

- **Stay relaxed**
- **Use wrist control (not arms)**
- **Keep palms down and elbows at sides**

FOR MORE SPECIFICS ON TECHNIQUE:

- 'Play Drums Now 1.0: Drumset Skill Basics'
- 'Play Drums Now 2.1: Sport / Rudiments'

All the exercises in the 'Play Drums Now' books are split up into the 4 'most typical musical feels'.

This is because almost 100% of modern music falls into one of these four categories - so as a drummer, it's strategic to **train your skills in all of them so you can be fully versatile.**

16TH NOTE FEEL

pulses grouped 4 at a time:

| o o o o | o o o o | o o o o | o o o o |
 1 e & a **2** e & a **3** e & a **4** e & a

8TH TRIPLET FEEL

pulses grouped 3 at a time:

| o o o | o o o | o o o | o o o |
 1 & a **2** & a **3** & a **4** & a

6/8 TIME FEEL

pulses grouped 6 at a time:

| o o o o o o | o o o o o o |
 1 & 2 & 3 & **4** & 5 & 6 &

SWUNG 16TH FEEL

pulses grouped in a 'shuffle':

|o_oo_o|o_oo_o|o_oo_o|o_oo_o|
 1 _e&_a **2** _e&_a **3** _e&_a **4** _e&_a

Find example songs in each feel on Spotify, by searching these playlists:

'DRUMS 16th feel'   'DRUMS Swung 16th feel'
'DRUMS 8th triplet feel'   'DRUMS 6/8 time feel'

READING THE NOTATION IN THIS BOOK

For the sake of clarity, **the Play Drums Now training materials use this style of notation:**

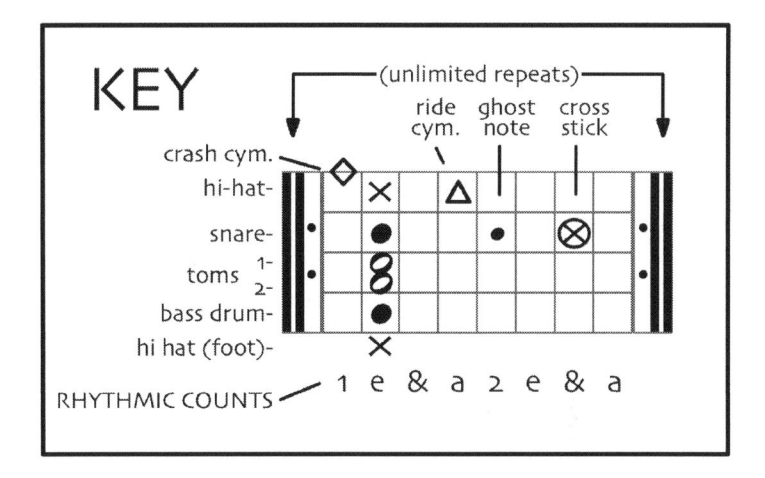

KEY — (unlimited repeats) — crash cym., hi-hat, ride cym., ghost note, cross stick, snare, toms 1-2, bass drum, hi hat (foot) — RHYTHMIC COUNTS: 1 e & a 2 e & a

This is used to make it easy to see the spacing of the rhythms in music.

UNLIMITED REPEATS

Repeat/loop the pattern as many times as you want without stopping. (Usually repeat signs mean 'play the section twice, then continue on'.)

CLEAR TOM NOTES

Usually 'open' noteheads are used for half- and whole- notes, but since drummers rarely need those sizes, they are used here to clearly distinguish the toms from the snare and bass.

TYPICAL DRUMSET NOTATION (USED IN OTHER BOOKS)

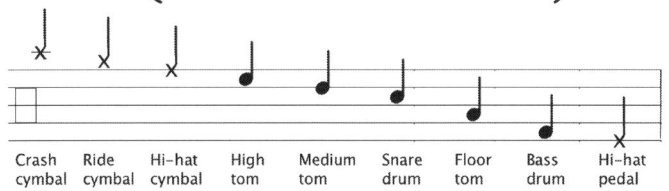

Crash cymbal, Ride cymbal, Hi-hat cymbal, High tom, Medium tom, Snare drum, Floor tom, Bass drum, Hi-hat pedal

Most other sheet music, method books, transcriptions etc. use this key. ^

SONG STRUCTURE SPECIFICS

SONGS ARE BUILT IN 'SECTIONS'.

Sections like **'verse', 'chorus', 'bridge',** etc. are the building blocks of modern songs.

There are usually about 5-20 of these sections in a typical song.

Drum parts are easy to create when you match your playing to the sections of the song.

A good drum part is supposed to highlight the progression of song sections, by accentuating the <u>changes in intensity</u> between them.

Many song structures* are provided in this book for you to follow while playing along, and get to know the layout of each song.

*(The song structures provided in this book are not transcriptions, just observed guidelines, and therefore may not have accurate section names or other details).

SONG SECTIONS, DEFINED

- **INTRO, OUTRO** - beginning and ending sections of the song, usually instrumental.
- **VAMP** - instrumental section
- **VERSE** - lyrical section, usually different lyrics for each verse.
- **CHORUS** - 'main' lyrical section of the song, usually same lyrics every chorus.
- **PRE-CHORUS** - right before chorus, more intense section of verse
- **POST-CHORUS** - right after chorus, extension of chorus vibe
- **BRIDGE** - different than verse and chorus, usually happens in second half of a song
- **SOLO** - usually same vibe as a verse or chorus, with an instrument soloing
- **HEAD** - (jazz music) the main 'song' part of any jazz music - usually played near the beginning and end of the song, with instrumental solos in-between

- **BREAK** - some or all instruments stop playing for a period of time
- **HITS** - most or all instruments play a short rhythm or series of notes together

'FOUR MEASURES' IS THE STANDARD UNIT OF CONSTRUCTION IN MUSIC.

This is true of nearly all music.

Chord progressions, melodies, lyrical phrases, and all instrumental parts tend to be created in a **four-measure pattern length**.

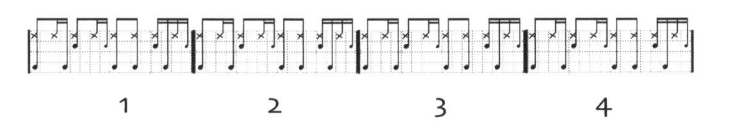

1   2   3   4

This is a natural cycle that feels good, predictable and grounded to most people.

Each song section (verse, chorus, etc.) is often made from 2-4 of these 'units' (8, 12, or 16 measures total), Sometimes they go longer or shorter.

All the suggested drum parts in this book are four-measure loops.

Drummers often play crash cymbals at the beginning of one of these loops and sometimes a fill at the end, depending on the style and intensity of the music.

OCCASIONAL CHANGES TO THE '4-MEASURE' CONSTRUCTION ARE COMMON.

Since 'four measures' has become so predictable, it sometimes sounds good to add an 'extra measure' or 'shortened section' to the music.

Pay attention to these changes in the provided song structures, so you can play along perfectly with the music and sound like a pro!

PLAYING SONG STRUCTURES

DRUMMERS PLAY A SECTION AT A TIME (VERSE, CHORUS, ETC.)

EVERY SECTION OF A SONG has a certain sound and a certain intensity level.

A GOOD DRUM PART MATCHES THE INTENSITY OF EACH SONG-SECTION (one level for the verse, one for the chorus, one for the bridge, etc.)

Some songs stay with the same vibe the whole way through, and the groove never has to change… but when the song vibe DOES change, the drum part **should abruptly change to a different intensity level** (or different groove altogether) when the section changes.

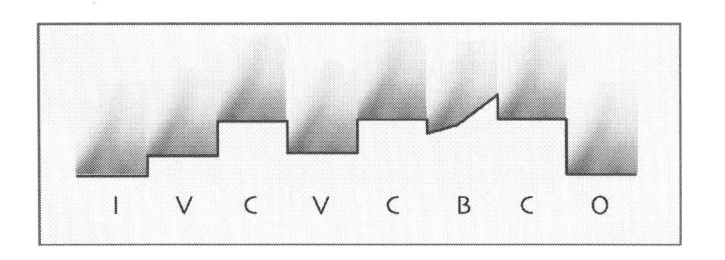

SONG STRUCTURE IS OFTEN PREDICTABLE

DRUMMERS ARE LUCKY - we don't have to deal with 'notes' or 'chords', so there's no danger of ever hitting a wrong note!

All we have to know is the order of song sections, which follows a similar recipe in 90% of popular music so it's predictable to a certain degree.

Besides possibly an intro, outro, and other additional sections, most modern songs have at least these core elements (in this order):

SONG 'CORE'

- **VERSE, CHORUS, VERSE, CHORUS**
- **BRIDGE (OR SOLO)**
- **CHORUS**

LEARN A SONG'S STRUCTURE AND FOLLOW IT

If you know the structure and general intensity levels of a song, you can do a pretty good job drumming to it.

So step one in playing with a song is listening to it. It's easy to remember a song's structure when you've heard the song enough to be familiar with it.

A DRUMMER'S JOB IS TO MAKE THE SONG STRUCTURE OBVIOUS BY EXAGGERATING THE INTENSITY LEVELS IN THE MUSIC.

The main goal of a good drum part is to decorate the song with an appealing rollercoaster of rising and falling 'percussive intensity'.

Songs often start with a medium intensity, drop to a low intensity for the first verse, then build up to a higher intensity for the chorus.

If you play those intensity levels really distinctly from each other, the music will have a really obvious flow to it, and the audience will feel like they're along for the ride.

THIS BOOK PROVIDES IDEAL TRAINING FOR DRUMMERS TO SWITCH GEARS BETWEEN VARIOUS INTENSITY LEVELS.

THERE IS ONE 'SIMPLE RECIPE' FOR INTENSITY:

YOUR ATTITUDE WHILE PLAYING.

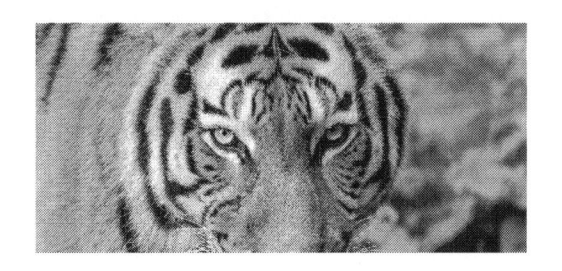

Of course, there are many specific ways to create a 'high-intensity' or a 'low-intensity' groove.

GENERAL GUIDELINES FOR INTENSITY

HIGH INTENSITY	vs.	LOW INTENSITY
• loud volume		quiet volume
• washy/sustained		tight/controlled
• mixed pitches		clear pitches
• low frequencies		high frequencies
• faster notes		slower notes
• sharp 'attack'		mellow 'attack'

For example, crash cymbals usually add a nice explosive touch and keep the energy high.

Playing a groove at high volume on a ride cymbal or loose hi-hats gives a washier, more intense sound.

Adding lots of fills keeps things exciting and high-energy.

WHICH SONGS TO LEARN / JAM WITH?

The songs chosen for this book are ideal to train with - they cover a wide base of popular tempos, across all four typical feels of music.

The following resources will also help you:

- **the 'POPULAR TEMPOS'** (following page) shows you the most common ranges of song tempos, so you can learn to play with those.

- **the 'TEMPO LIST'** helps you find songs at the tempo you need, in each feel.

- **the 'SPOTIFY PLAYLISTS FOR DRUMMERS'** provide a wide variety of drummable songs in each 'feel' of music.

SPOTIFY PLAYLISTS FOR DRUMMERS

There are several useful playlists created for drummers. Find them all on Spotify by first searching for any of these four:

- DRUMS 16th feel
- DRUMS Swung 16th feel
- DRUMS 8th triplet feel
- DRUMS 6/8 time feel

These playlists were created for drummers to jam with, as well as find new songs to enjoy and/or learn. They are continually being updated with new music discoveries.

THE TEMPO LIST

visit www.playdrumsnow.com/tempos

This resource I've been working on has hundreds of songs total, split into different feels. It's highly subjective based on my own taste in 'drummable' songs, and is definitely a work in progress.

MEASURE YOUR VERSATILITY

As a fun test, set the playback to random on any of these playlists and try to jam with whatever comes up!

POPULAR SONG TEMPOS (ANALYSIS)

This is a visual that represents **the popularity of each tempo** with the height of a bar. It was compiled with data from over 600 songs, to be as accurate as possible.

You will want to be comfortable playing grooves / fills / songs in all the most popular tempo zones, so you can play across the largest possible range of music.

6/8 > 8TH TRIPLET > SWUNG 16TH
(part of the same 'feel' spectrum)

Above a certain tempo, the 6/8 feel BECOMES the 8th triplet feel. Above another certain tempo, the 8th triplet feel BECOMES the swung 16th feel.

The three 'connected' feels are **all based on a grouping of 3 counts**, so they are just different parts of one spectrum - much like how water turns to ice at low temperatures and steam at high temperatures, but it's all the same element.

Many songs are in the 'crossover zones' and could be interpreted as more than one feel.

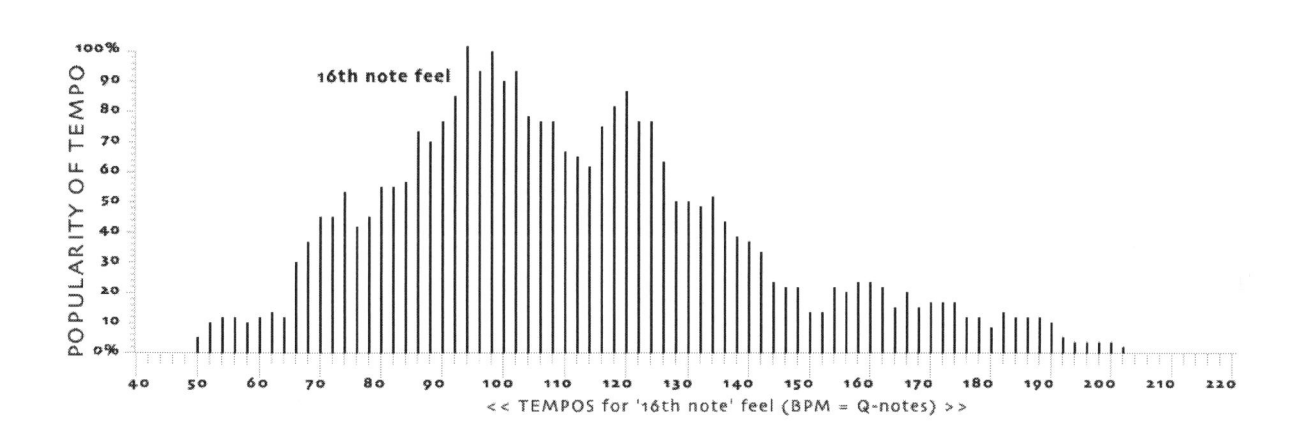

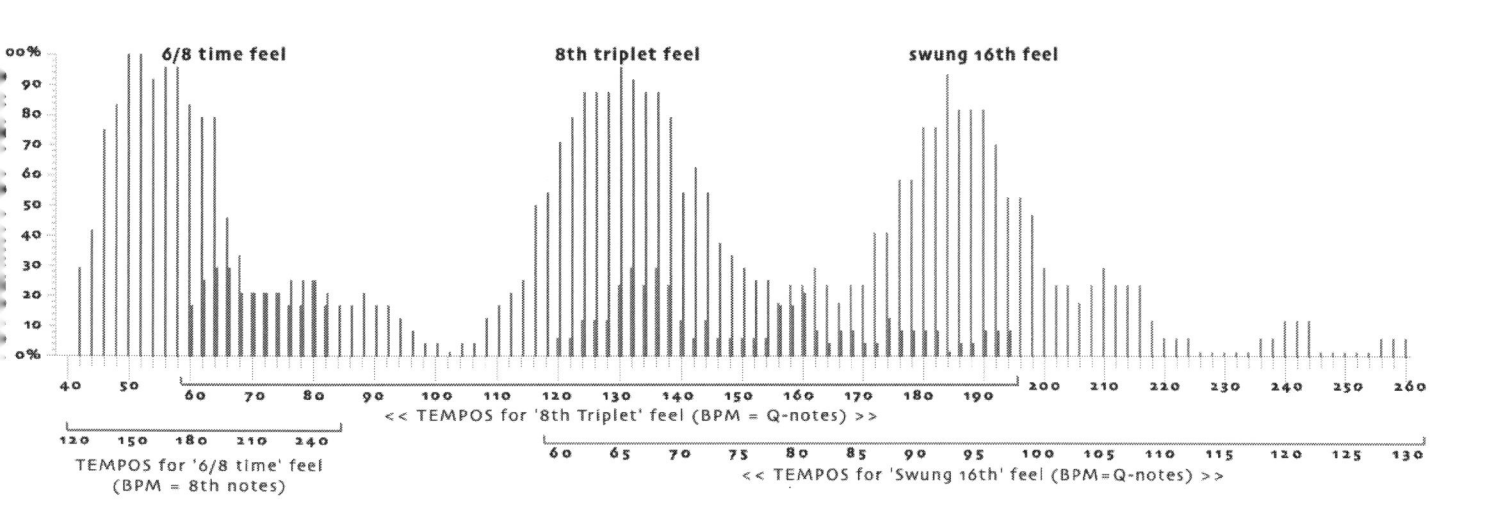

TIPS FOR PLAYING WITH SONGS

YOU CAN PLAY ALONG TO SONGS IN TWO WAYS:

1) trying to sound good with the music
(treating the song as a piece of musical art)

2) not caring how you sound with the music
(treating the song to be a metronomic backdrop for your own agenda).

BOTH WAYS ARE REALLY VALUABLE FOR YOUR TRAINING.

This book uses a mix of these two. ^

The suggested drum parts in this book are intended to sound good with the music, but are designed **more for training drummers** than for making the song sound its best.

For example, the part often indicates MORE switching between A, B, and C parts than the song necessarily needs. This is done to help equip drummers with the skill of making transitions around the drumset.

Plus the suggested grooves are generally NOT what the drummers are playing in the songs.

LEARNING ACCURATE DRUM PARTS IS REALLY VALUABLE

Anytime you learn to play another drummer's recorded part note for note, you're essentially stepping into their shoes. This is a quick way to learn from some incredibly skilled and intelligent artists.

Your mind might learn from some of their creative decisions, and your body might pick up some of their movement habits / phrases.

You can either learn songs:

- **by reading -** get a transcription of the song, watch a YouTube drum cover, or have a drum instructor transcribe it… then work on rehearsing it piece by piece

- **by ear -** listen to the song and imitate the drum part until you master it

- **…or both (ideal) -** learn from the transcription AND listen to exactly HOW the drummer is playing their part.

LISTENING IS <u>THE KEY</u>

Listening closely to the music you're playing WHILE PLAYING IT is by far the most valuable musical skill. Practice it ALL THE TIME!!

PLAY LIKE YOU'RE PERFORMING

How you play is important, because your job when performing is to ENTERTAIN.

Entertaining an audience is relatively simple - the main 'secret' is <u>HAVE LOTS OF FUN, VISIBLY</u>.

Enjoy yourself and so will the audience, because fun is contagious. Therefore it's important to practice playing with this vibe in general, so it comes naturally to you.

LEARN MORE SONGS

It's good to continue expanding your 'playable vocabulary' of songs. The more songs you know how to play, the easier they are to learn!

USEFUL APPS / WEBSITES

- **Moises** - removes drums (and other parts) from any song. Try playing with drumless versions of songs, for more intense training!
- **GetSongBPM.com** - allows you to look up music (with tempo listed) by title, artist, genre, bpm, etc.

HAVE FUN WITH DECORATING YOUR DRUM PART

Add plenty of crashes, and experiment with fills a lot until you feel confident about knowing where and how to place them.

SHORTER FILLS = LESS INTENSE
LONGER FILLS = MORE INTENSE

Save the LONGER fills for important transition moments in the song, like going from the verse to the chorus.

Remember - YOU DON'T HAVE TO SOUND LIKE THE DRUMS IN THE SONG.

Use your own ears and judgment to determine what fits best with any songs you play along with!

FIND THESE SONGS ON THE SPOTIFY PLAYLISTS

Every song used in this book is in the appropriate DRUMS playlist according to its 'feel'. The 'clean' versions are included for any of these songs with explicit lyrics. Look for:

'DRUMS 16th feel' **'DRUMS Swung 16th feel'**
'DRUMS 8th triplet feel' **'DRUMS 6/8 time feel'**

INSTRUCTIONS: SONG PARTS FOR DRUMS

vv (follow these instructions for each song part)

EXERCISE 1 - Learn the 'song part'

1) Play the groove and all fills until they are familiar (or ideally, memorized).

2) Play through the entire song part. Do each line twice (once for each fill option), before going to the next line.

EXERCISE 2 - Play with the songs

For each song,

1) Listen to the song while reading its structure. Notice the intensity level of each section, as well as how the song starts and ends and any other useful details.

2) Play along with the music, using the suggested parts in the suggested order. Practice this until it feels easy.

3) Modify your part to fit the song better, based on your judgment.

4) GOAL: Learn to play the song without reading any of the parts.

**NOTE: THE FOLLOWING SONG INFO IS NOT 'CORRECT'

THESE ARE NOT TRANSCRIPTIONS.

The suggested drum parts are not based on any song(s) in particular. Any 'section names' and 'song structures' are simply approximate observations to help you play along with the songs in a meaningful way.

The provided parts are simply practice to help you experience GENERALLY what kind of drumming works in music, and are often deliberately different from the original drum part.

TIPS

- **EXTRA MEASURES -** When there are 1, 2, or 3 extra measures in a section, use the end part of the 4-measure loop. That way there will be a fill at the end.

- **BREAKS - indicated by a dash (—)** Sometimes the music stops or certain instruments cut out for a measure or two. You can choose how to approach these - either play a groove or fill during the break, or stop playing until the end of the break.

- **SUBSTITUTE OTHER GROOVES/FILLS -** Feel free to try any grooves and fills you want with these songs. It's good to get practice experimenting with possibilities.

  - Use Play Drums Now books 2.3 and 2.4 for tons of groove and fill ideas!

  - BONUS POINTS - Try using a different groove for each section of a song, to achieve a sharper change in intensity between them.

SONG PARTS FOR DRUMS
SECTION 1:
16th Note Feel

- SLOW SONGS (70-90 BPM) - P.16
- MEDIUM-SLOW SONGS (90-110 BPM) - P.18
- MEDIUM-FAST SONGS (110-140 BPM) - P.22
- FAST SONGS (140-160 BPM) - P.26

PLAY DRUMS NOW
THE ULTIMATE DRUMSET TRAINING PROGRAM

EXAMPLE: USING THE DRUM PARTS AND SONG STRUCTURES TOGETHER

SUGGESTED DRUM SEQUENCES
(from p.15)

+

SONG STRUCTURE #1 >>
(more structures on p.16)

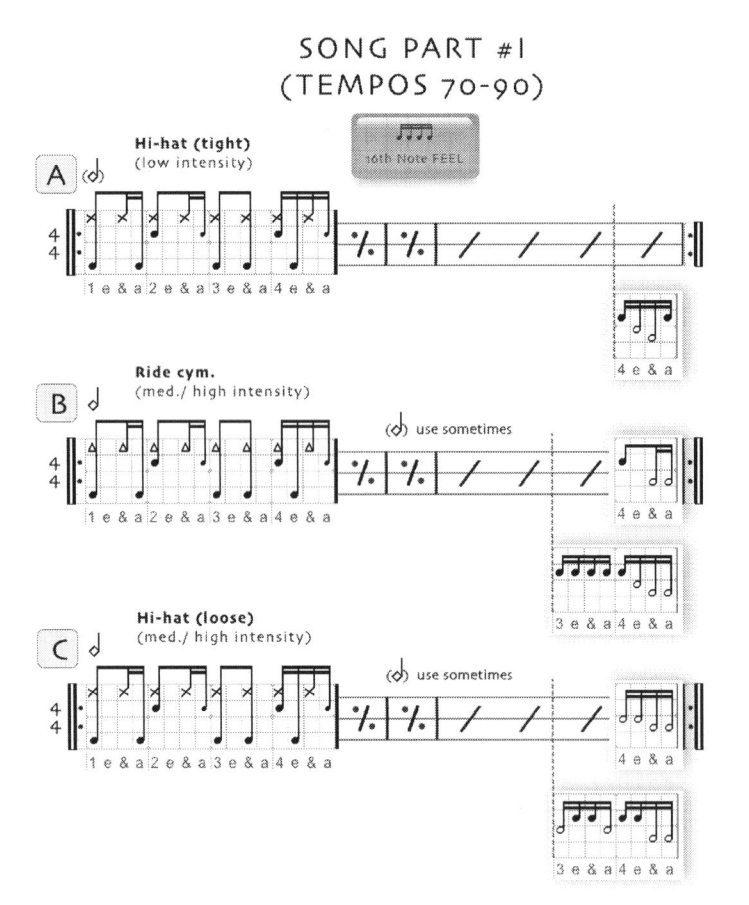

SONG PART #1
(TEMPOS 70-90)

A Hi-hat (tight) (low intensity) — 16th Note FEEL

B Ride cym. (med./high intensity)

C Hi-hat (loose) (med./high intensity)

"Do what you do' (Mudvayne)
(2008) tempo = 83 bpm

SECTION NAME	PART TO PLAY	NOTES
Vamp	A (x 1)	
Verse 1	A (x 2)	
Chorus	C (x 2)	+1 measure
Verse 2	A (x 2)	
Chorus	C (x 2)	
Bridge	C (x 2)	
Gtr. solo	B (x 2)	
Chorus	C (x 2)	
Bridge	C (x 2)	*hits next measure

(EXAMPLE DRUM PART #1)

*Feel free to substitute other grooves and fills.

SONG PART #1
(TEMPOS 70-90)

(INSTRUCTIONS, p.12)

SONG STRUCTURES >>

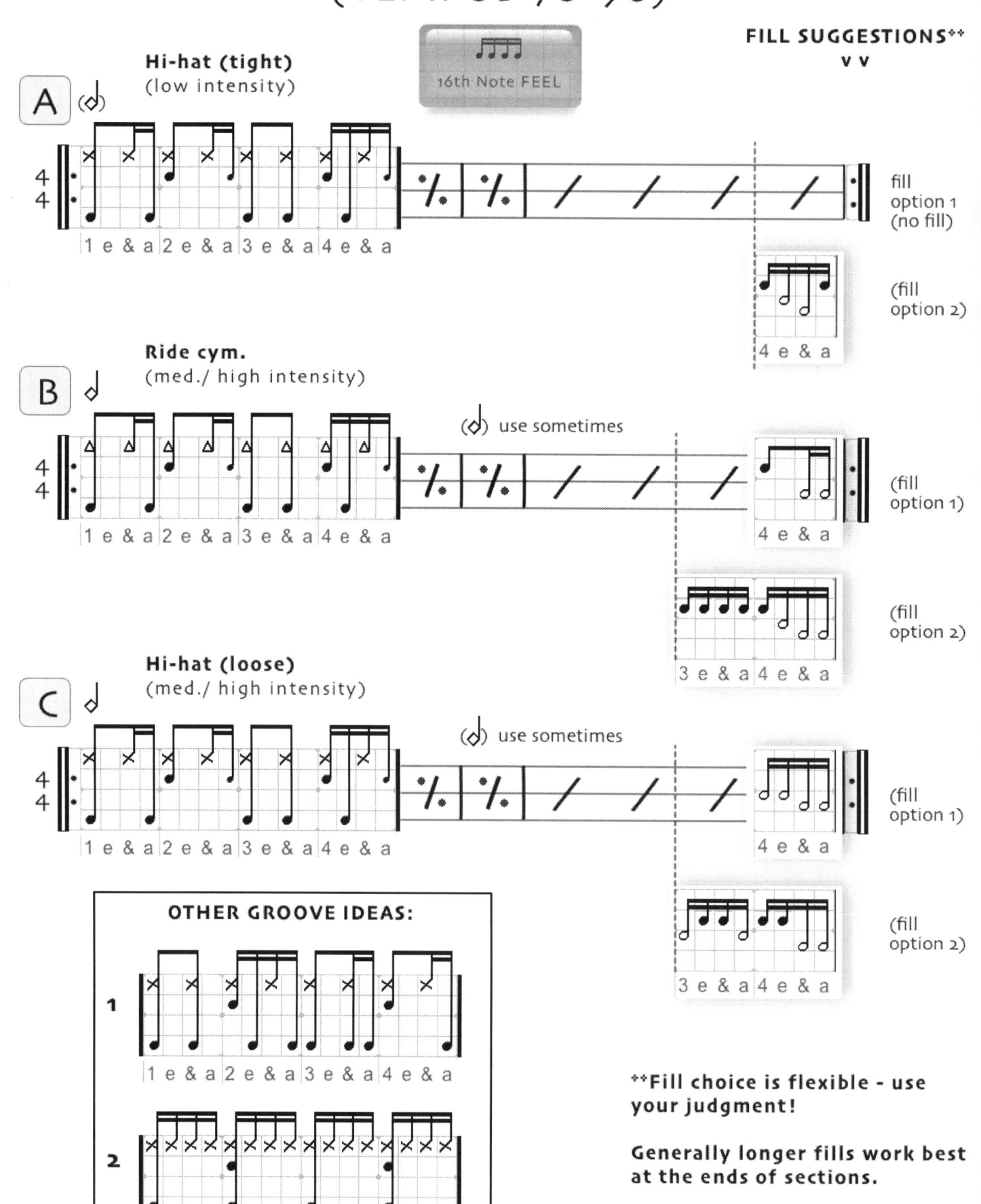

FILL SUGGESTIONS*
v v

16th Note FEEL

A Hi-hat (tight) (low intensity)

fill option 1 (no fill)

(fill option 2)

B Ride cym. (med./ high intensity)

(♩) use sometimes

(fill option 1)

(fill option 2)

C Hi-hat (loose) (med./ high intensity)

(♩) use sometimes

(fill option 1)

(fill option 2)

OTHER GROOVE IDEAS:

1

2

Fill choice is flexible - use your judgment!

Generally longer fills work best at the ends of sections.

16

LOVE SONG (311)

*original version by The Cure
(2004) tempo = 70 bpm

SECTION NAME	PART TO PLAY	NOTES
Vamp	A (x 2)	
Verse 1	A (x 2)	
Vamp	B (x 1)	
Verse 2	A (x 2)	
Chorus	B (x 1)	+3 measures
Gtr. solo	B (x 4)	
Break	(4 measures)	
Verse 3	A (x 1)	
Chorus	B (x 1)	+3 measures

BLURRY (PUDDLE OF MUDD)

(2001) tempo = 78 bpm

SECTION NAME	PART TO PLAY	NOTES
Intro	— (x 2 measures)	
	A (2 measures)	
Vamp	A (x 1)	
Verse 1	A (x 4)	
Chorus	C (x 2)	
Verse 2	A (x 4)	
Chorus	C (x 3)	
Bridge	B (x 2)	
Chorus	C (x 4)	
Outro	A (x 1)	+3 measures

DON'T TELL (ROYAL BLOOD)

(2017) tempo = 70 bpm

SECTION NAME	PART TO PLAY	NOTES
Vamp	B (x 1)	+2 measures
Verse	A (x 2)	
Chorus	B (x 1)	+2 measures
Verse	A (x 2)	
Chorus	B (x 1)	+2 measures
Bridge	C (x 2)	
Gtr. solo	B (x 2)	
Chorus	B (x 2)	+2 measures

DOIN' TIME (SUBLIME)

(1996) tempo = 81 bpm

SECTION NAME	PART TO PLAY	NOTES
Intro	— (x 3 measures)	
	A (1 measure)	
Chorus	A (x 2)	
Verse	A (x 2)	
Chorus	B (x 2)	
Verse	A (x 2)	
Chorus	B (x 2)	
Verse	A (x 2)	
Bridge	A (x 2)	
Chorus	B (x 6)	*fade out

*Feel free to substitute other grooves and fills.

SONG PART #2
(TEMPOS 90-110)

(INSTRUCTIONS, p.12)

SONG STRUCTURES >>

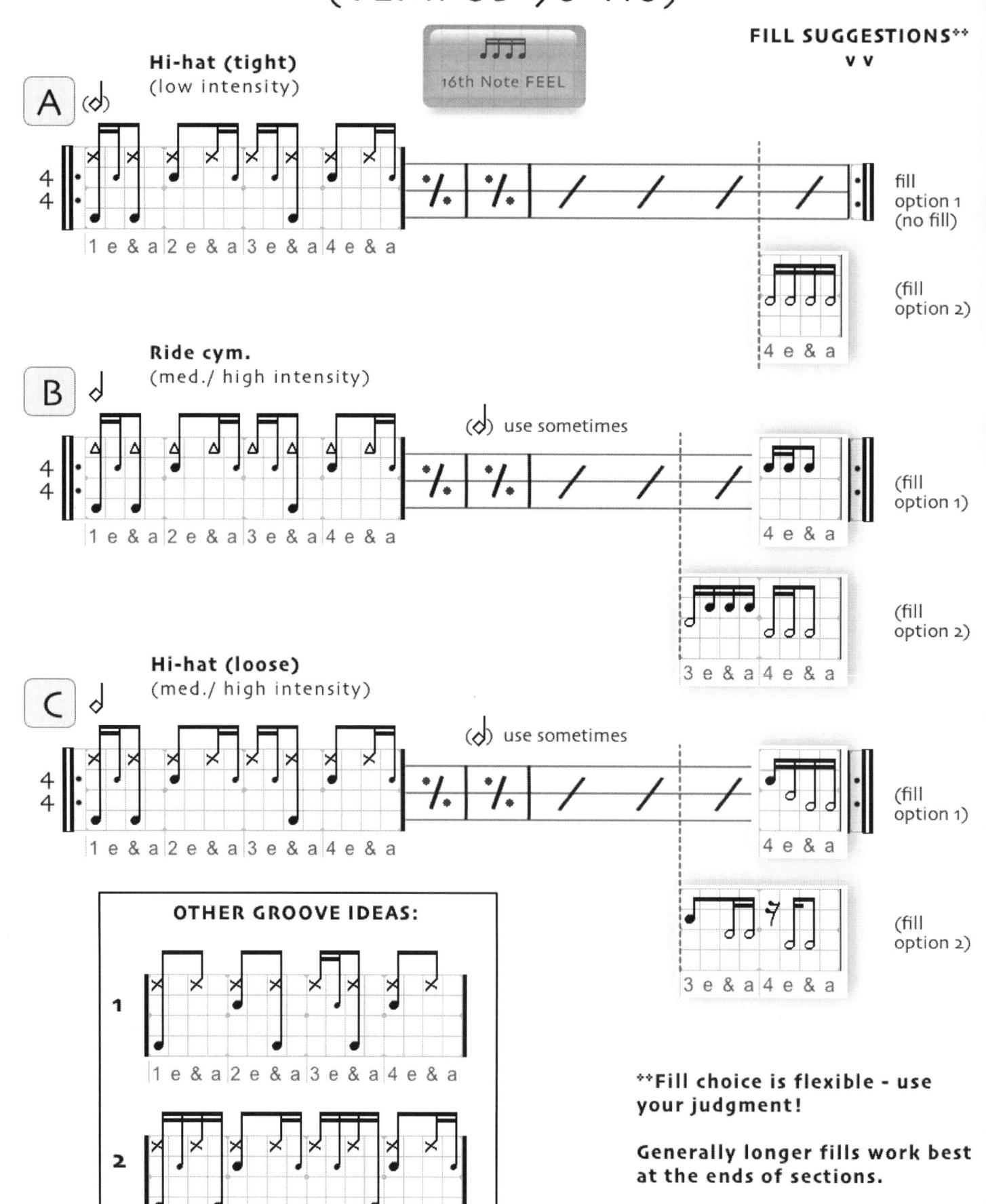

FILL SUGGESTIONS**
v v

16th Note FEEL

A Hi-hat (tight) (low intensity)

1 e & a 2 e & a 3 e & a 4 e & a

fill option 1 (no fill)

(fill option 2)
4 e & a

B Ride cym. (med./ high intensity)

(♪) use sometimes

1 e & a 2 e & a 3 e & a 4 e & a

(fill option 1)
4 e & a

(fill option 2)
3 e & a 4 e & a

C Hi-hat (loose) (med./ high intensity)

(♪) use sometimes

1 e & a 2 e & a 3 e & a 4 e & a

(fill option 1)
4 e & a

(fill option 2)
3 e & a 4 e & a

OTHER GROOVE IDEAS:

1
1 e & a 2 e & a 3 e & a 4 e & a

2
1 e & a 2 e & a 3 e & a 4 e & a

**Fill choice is flexible - use your judgment!

Generally longer fills work best at the ends of sections.

SHOW ME HOW TO LIVE (AUDIOSLAVE)

(2002) tempo = 90 bpm

SECTION NAME	PART TO PLAY	NOTES
Vamp	A (x 2)	
	C (x 2)	
Verse 1	A (x 4)	
Chorus	C (x 2)	
Verse 2	A (x 2)	
Chorus	C (x 2)	
Gtr. solo	B (x 2)	
Break	— (1 measure)	
Verse 3	A (x 4)	*2nd half is snare roll
Chorus	C (x 4)	

DARK NECESSITIES (RED HOT CHILI PEPPERS)

(2016) tempo = 92 bpm

SECTION NAME	PART TO PLAY	NOTES
Intro	— (x 4 measures)	
Vamp	A (x 4)	
Verse 1	A (x 4)	
Chorus	B (x 2)	
Vamp	A (x 1)	
Verse 2	A (x 2)	
Chorus	B (x 2)	
Bridge	A (x 2)	+1 measure break
Verse 3	A (x 2)	
Chorus	B (x 2)	
Gtr. solo	C (x 4)	

MRS. ORLEANS (TROMBONE SHORTY, KID ROCK)

(2011) tempo = 93 bpm

SECTION NAME	PART TO PLAY	NOTES
Vamp	A (x 2)	*play groove on toms
	A (x 1)	
Verse 1	A (x 2)	
Chorus	B (x 2)	
Vamp	A (x 1)	
Verse 2	A (x 2)	
Chorus	B (x 2)	
Verse 3	A (x 2)	
	C (x 1)	
Chorus	B (x 4)	

MIDNIGHT RIDER (ALLMAN BROTHERS BAND)

(1970) tempo = 95 bpm

SECTION NAME	PART TO PLAY	NOTES
Intro	— (x 2 measures)	
Vamp	A (x 1)	
Verse/Chorus	A (x 2)	
Vamp	A (x 1)	
Verse/Chorus	A (x 2)	
Vamp	A (x 1)	
Gtr. solo	B (x 2)	+3 measures
Vamp	A (x 1)	
Verse 2	A (x 1)	+2 measures
Chorus	A (x 5)	*fade out

IN THE END (LINKIN PARK)

(2000) tempo = 100 bpm

SECTION NAME	PART TO PLAY	NOTES
Intro	— (x 8 measures)	
Verse 1	A (x 4)	
Chorus	C (x 2)	
Verse 1	A (x 4)	
Chorus	C (x 2)	+1 measure
Bridge	A (x 2)	
	C (x 2)	
Chorus	C (x 2)	
Outro	— (x 8 measures)	

WISH I KNEW YOU (THE REVIVALISTS)

(2015) tempo = 101 bpm

SECTION NAME	PART TO PLAY	NOTES
Intro	— (x 4 measures)	
Verse 1	A (x 4)	+1 measure
Chorus	A (x 4)	+1 measure
Vamp	A (x 1)	
Verse 2	A (x 4)	+1 measure
Chorus	A (x 4)	+1 measure
Vamp	A (x 1)	
Bridge	A (x 2)	
	— (4 measures)	
Chorus	A (x 4)	+1 measure

LEAVE ME ALONE (I DON'T KNOW HOW BUT THEY FOUND ME)

(2020) tempo = 104 bpm

SECTION NAME	PART TO PLAY	NOTES
Intro	— (x 1 measure)	
Vamp	A (x 1)	
Verse 1	A (x 2)	
Chorus	B (x 4)	
Vamp	A (x 1)	
Verse 2	A (x 2)	
Chorus	B (x 4)	
Bridge	— (12 measures)	
Vamp	A (x 1)	
Chorus	B (x 4)	
Vamp	B (x 2)	

BRICK HOUSE (THE COMMODORES)

(1977) tempo = 106 bpm

SECTION NAME	PART TO PLAY	NOTES
Vamp	A (x 2)	
Chorus	A (x 3)	
Verse 1	A (x 2)	
Chorus	A (x 3)	
Verse 2	A (x 2)	
Chorus	A (x 2)	
Bridge	B (x 2)	
Chorus	A (x 2)	
Bridge	B (x 2)	
Break	— (x 4 measures)	
Outro	A (x 2)	*fade out

*Feel free to substitute other grooves and fills.

SONG PART #3
(TEMPOS 110-140)

(INSTRUCTIONS, p.12)

SONG STRUCTURES >>

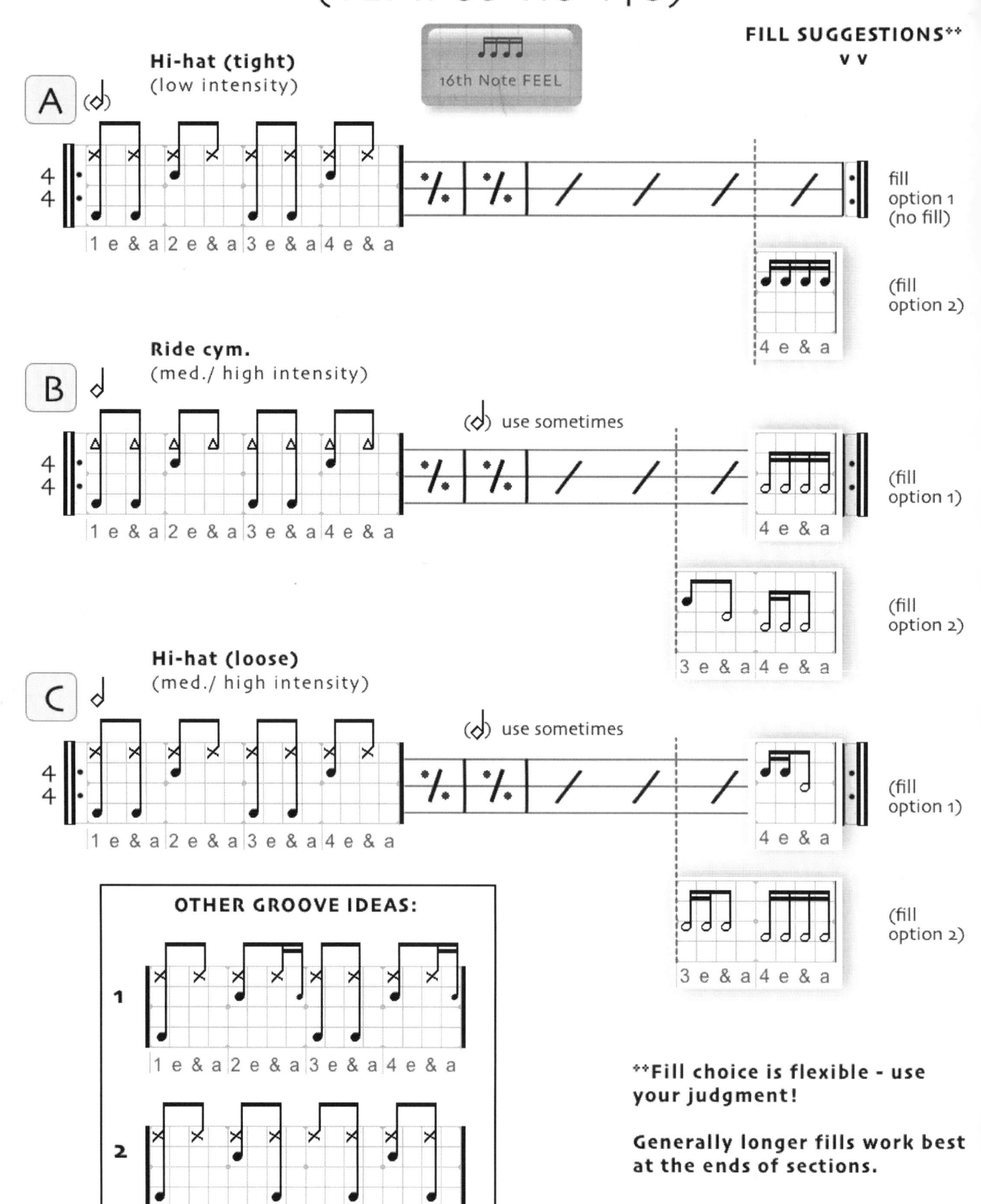

FILL SUGGESTIONS*
v v

16th Note FEEL

A Hi-hat (tight) (low intensity)

fill option 1 (no fill)

(fill option 2)

B Ride cym. (med./ high intensity)

(♩) use sometimes

(fill option 1)

(fill option 2)

C Hi-hat (loose) (med./ high intensity)

(♩) use sometimes

(fill option 1)

(fill option 2)

OTHER GROOVE IDEAS:

1

2

Fill choice is flexible - use your judgment!

Generally longer fills work best at the ends of sections.

ON TIME (DISCO BISCUITS)

(2010) tempo = 110 bpm

SECTION NAME	PART TO PLAY	NOTES
Vamp	A (x 2)	
Verse 1	A (x 4)	
Chorus	C (x 2)	
Vamp	A (x 2)	
Verse 2	A (x 4)	
Chorus	C (x 2)	
Break	— (1 measure)	
Bridge	B (x 4)	
Chorus	C (x 4)	
Vamp	A (x 1)	

CRIMINAL (THE REVIVALISTS)

(2012) tempo = 115 bpm

SECTION NAME	PART TO PLAY	NOTES
Intro	— (4 measures)	
Vamp	A (x 2)	
Verse 1	A (x 6)	
Chorus	C (x 2)	
Vamp	A (x 2)	
Verse 2	A (x 4)	
Chorus	C (x 2)	+1 measure
Gtr. solo	C (x 4)	
Break	— (16 measures)	
Verse 3	A (x 4)	
Chorus	C (x 4)	+1 measure
Sax solo	C (x 2)	+2 measures

LONG TRAIN RUNNIN' (THE DOOBIE BROTHERS)

(1973) tempo = 116 bpm

SECTION NAME	PART TO PLAY	NOTES
Intro	— (x 4 measures)	
Vamp	A (x 1)	
Verse 1	A (x 9)	
Solo	B (x 3)	
Verse 2	A (x 5)	
Break (pause)		
Outro	B (x 4)	*fade out

BILLIE JEAN (MICHAEL JACKSON)

(1982) tempo = 117 bpm

SECTION NAME	PART TO PLAY	NOTES
Intro	A (x 2 measures)	
Vamp	A (x 3)	
Verse 1	A (x 5)	
Pre-chorus	C (x 2)	
Chorus	A (x 3)	
Verse 2	A (x 7)	
Pre-chorus	C (x 2)	
Chorus	A (x 5)	
Pre-chorus	C (x 2)	
Chorus	A (x 5)	
Gtr. solo	C (x 2)	
Chorus	A (x 7)	*fade out

THE ONE I LOVE (R.E.M.)

(1987) tempo = 128 bpm

SECTION NAME	PART TO PLAY	NOTES
Vamp	C (x 2)	
Verse 1	A (x 2)	
	B (x 1)	
	A (x 1)	
Chorus	B (x 2)	
Verse 2	A (x 2)	
	B (x 1)	
	A (x 1)	
Chorus	B (x 2)	
Bridge	B (x 2)	
Verse 3	A (x 2)	
	B (x 1)	
	A (x 1)	
Chorus	B (x 4)	*slow ending

ROCK THE CASBAH (THE CLASH)

(1982) tempo = 130 bpm

SECTION NAME	PART TO PLAY	NOTES
Vamp	A (x 2)	
Verse 1	A (x 4)	
Chorus	B (x 2)	
Verse 2	A (x 4)	
Chorus	B (x 2)	
Verse 3	A (x 4)	
Chorus	B (x 2)	
Verse 4	A (x 4)	
Chorus	B (x 5)	*fade out

FREEZE ME
(DEATH FROM ABOVE 1979)

(2017) tempo = 130 bpm

SECTION NAME	PART TO PLAY	NOTES
Intro	— (x 8 measures)	
Vamp	B (x 2)	
Verse 1	A (x 4)	
Chorus	C (x 2)	
Vamp	B (x 2)	
Verse 2	A (x 4)	
Chorus	C (x 2)	
Bridge	A (x 1)	
	B (x 2)	
Break	— (x 4 measures	
Chorus	C (x 4)	

PANIC SWITCH
(SILVERSUN PICKUPS)

(2009) tempo = 132 bpm

SECTION NAME	PART TO PLAY	NOTES
Intro	— (x 4 measures)	
Vamp	C (x 6)	
Verse 1	A (x 4)	
Pre-chorus	C (x 2)	
Chorus	B (x 4)	
Vamp	C (x 2)	
Verse 2	A (x 4)	
Pre-chorus	C (x 2)	
Chorus	B (x 4)	
Break	— (x 16 measures)	
Pre-chorus	C (x 4)	
Bridge	C (x 2)	
Chorus	B (x 4)	
Outro	B (x 2)	

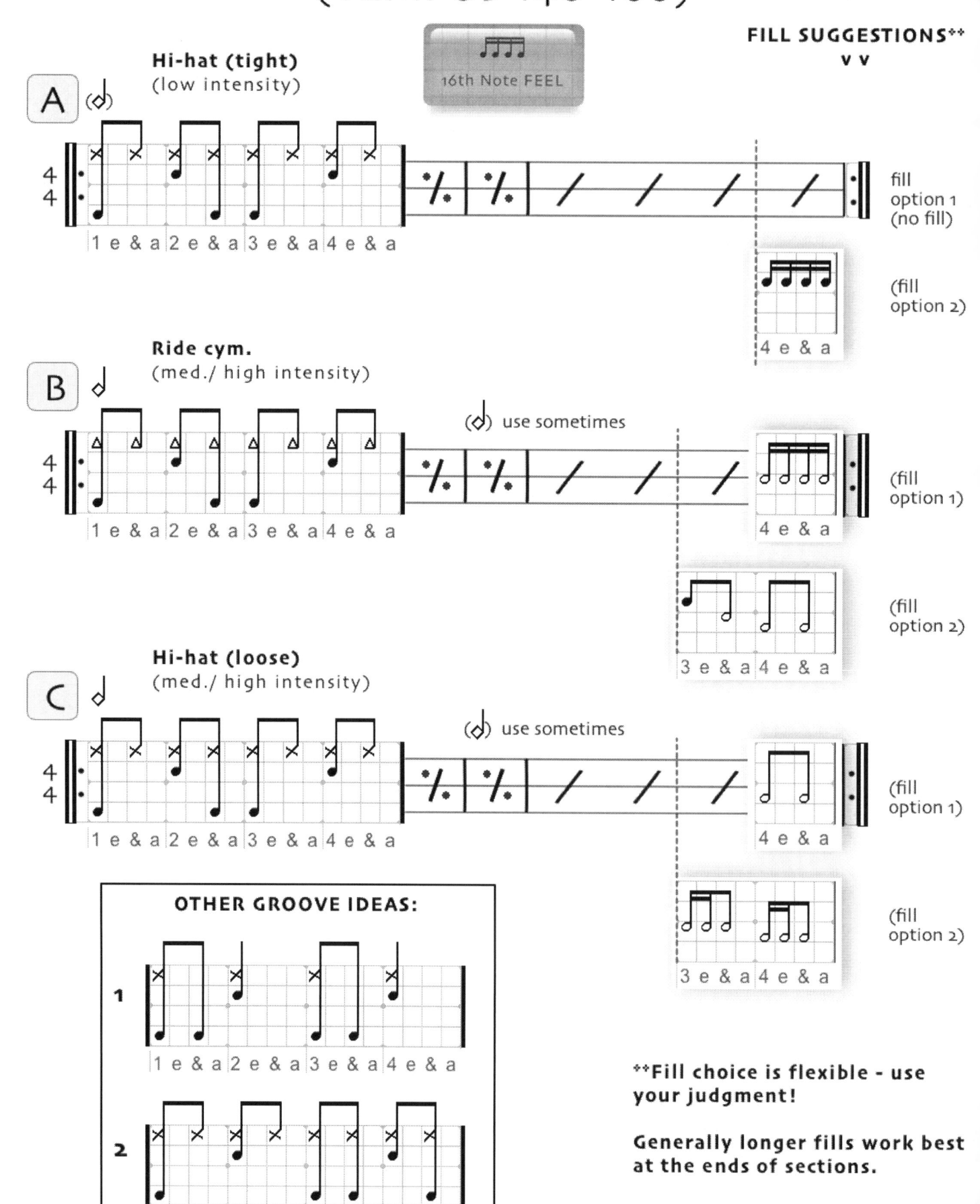

WHITE WEDDING (BILLY IDOL)

(1982) tempo = 147 bpm

SECTION NAME	PART TO PLAY	NOTES
Intro	— (1 measure)	
Vamp	A (x 4)	
Verse 1	A (x 3)	+2 measures
Chorus	C (x 3)	
Verse 2	A (x 3)	+2 measures
Chorus	C (x 2)	+2 measures
	C (x 1)	
Vamp	B (x 5)	
Verse 3	A (x 3)	+2 measures
Chorus	C (x 2)	+2 measures
	C (x 1)	
Bridge	A (x 4)	+2 measures
Chorus	C (x 3)	*fade out

OVERDRIVE (FOO FIGHTERS)

(2002) tempo = 157 bpm

SECTION NAME	PART TO PLAY	NOTES
Vamp	B (x 4)	
Verse 1	C (x 8)	
Chorus	B (x 5)	+2 measures
Verse 2	C (x 4)	
Chorus	B (x 4)	+2 measures
Gtr. solo	C (x 3)	
Verse 3	C (x 4)	*break last 2 measures
Chorus	B (x 3)	+2 measures
	B (x 5)	

WASTE A MOMENT (KINGS OF LEON)

(2016) tempo = 153 bpm

SECTION NAME	PART TO PLAY	NOTES
Intro	— (x 8 measures)	
Vamp	A (x 2)	
Verse 1	A (x 4)	
Chorus	C (x 2)	
Vamp	A (x 2)	
Verse 2	A (x 4)	
Chorus	C (x 4)	
Vamp	A (x 2)	
Vamp	C (x 1)	+2 measures
Chorus	C (x 4)	
Vamp	A (x 1)	

BREED (NIRVANA)

(1991) tempo = 159 bpm

SECTION NAME	PART TO PLAY	NOTES
Intro	— (x 8 measures)	
Vamp	C (x 2)	
Verse 1	C (x 4)	
Chorus	B (x 2)	
Post chorus	C (x 2)	
Verse 2	C (x 4)	
Chorus	B (x 2)	
Post chorus	C (x 2)	
Gtr. solo	C (x 4)	
Chorus	B (x 2)	
Post chorus	C (x 2)	

Part IV: Swung 16th FEEL

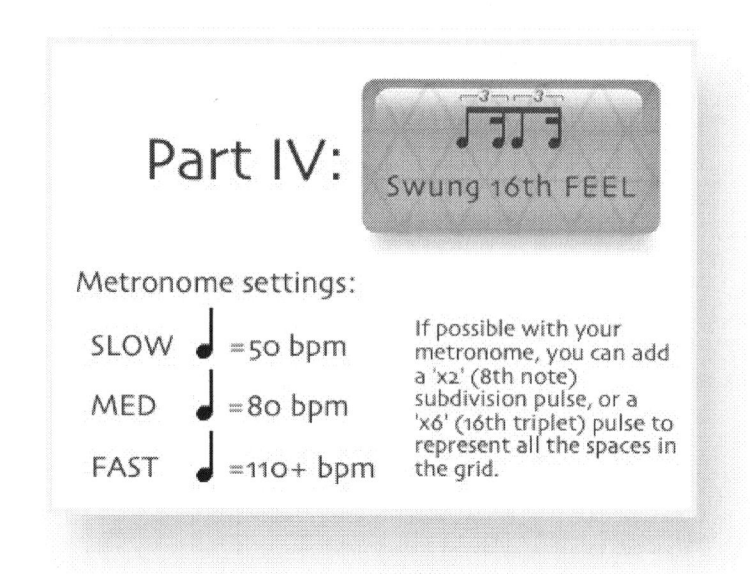

Metronome settings:

SLOW ♩ =50 bpm
MED ♩ =80 bpm
FAST ♩ =110+ bpm

If possible with your metronome, you can add a 'x2' (8th note) subdivision pulse, or a 'x6' (16th triplet) pulse to represent all the spaces in the grid.

To learn grooves in the 'Swung 16th Feel', read/play the '16th Feel' grooves again, and adjust the timing as shown below.

(Check out the song examples listed in the instructions, for clarity)

16th Note Feel

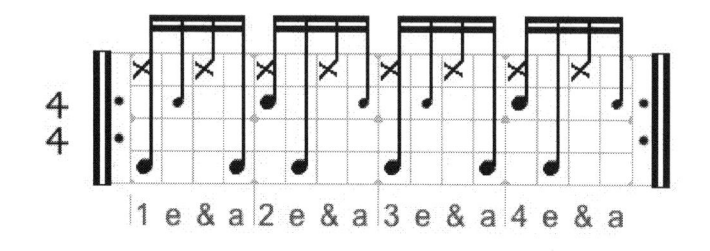

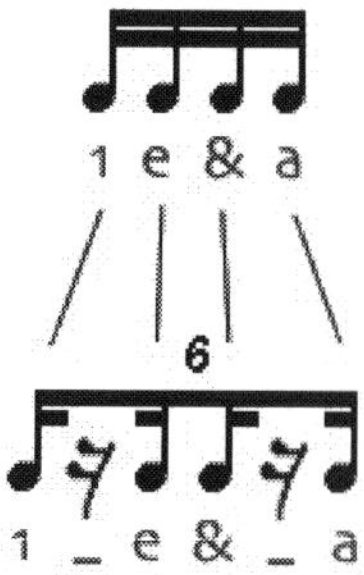

1 e & a 2 e & a 3 e & a 4 e & a

⬇

Swung 16th Note Feel

1 _ e & _ a 2 _ e & _ a 3 _ e & _ a 4 _ e & _ a

When counting vocally, instead of the steady sounding '1,e,&,a,2,e,&,a' it will sound more like '1 - e,& - a,2 - e,& - a'.

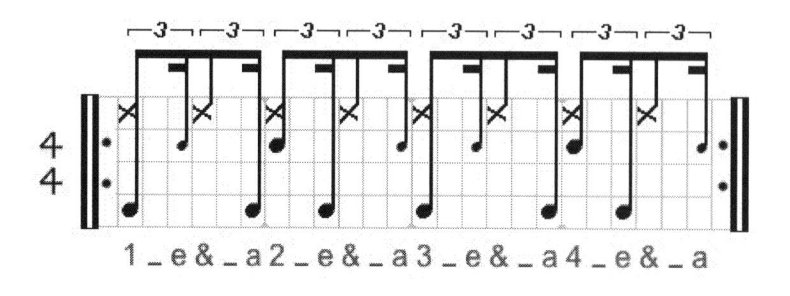

To 'swing' a 16th note pattern, each pair of 16th note counts gets widened, adding a space to the middle. The result is a rhythm that lines up with the first and third notes of triplets, but never uses the middle note.

SONG PARTS FOR DRUMS

SECTION IV:

Swung 16th Feel

- SLOW SONGS (70-90 BPM) - P.30
- FAST SONGS (90-110 BPM) - P.32

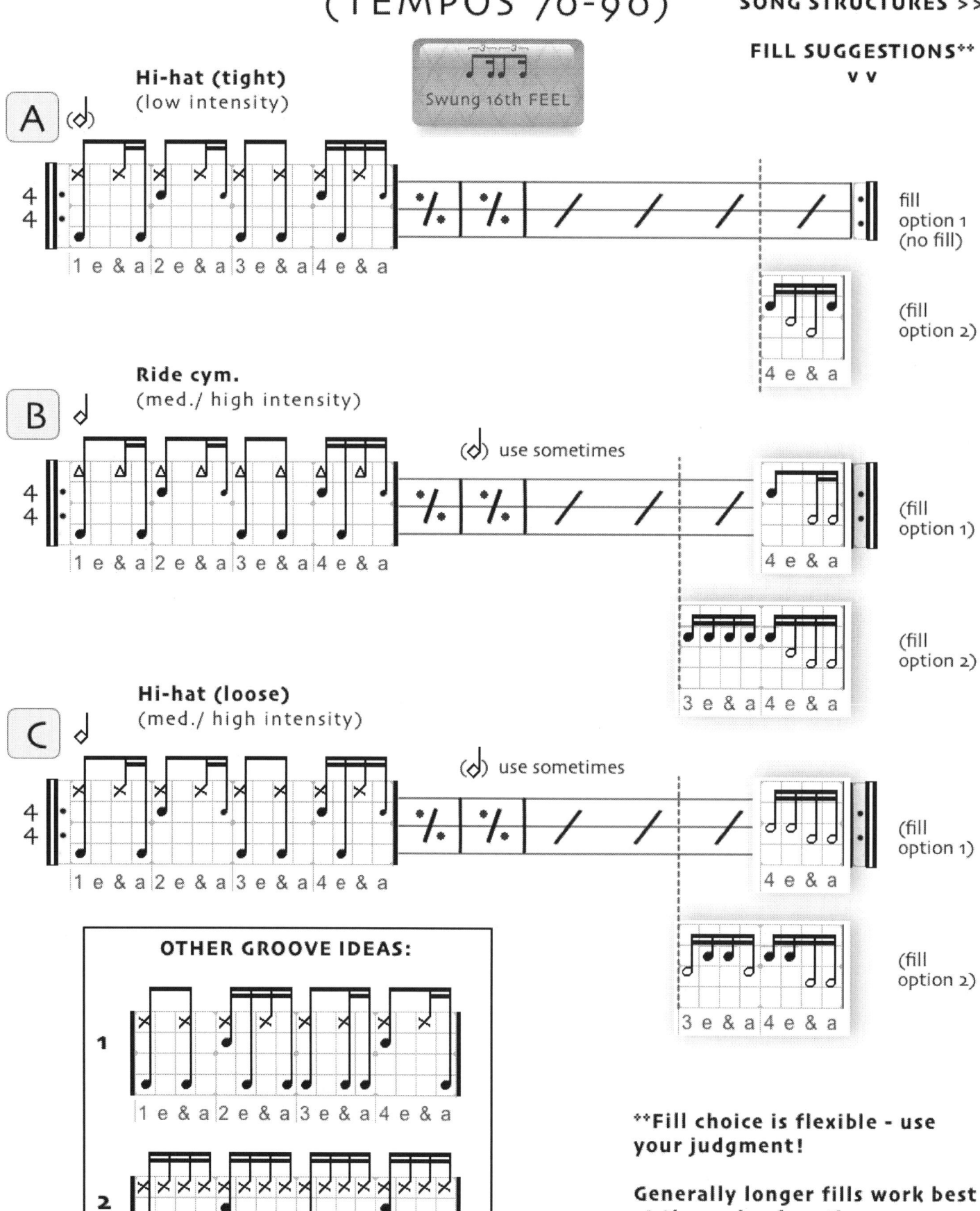

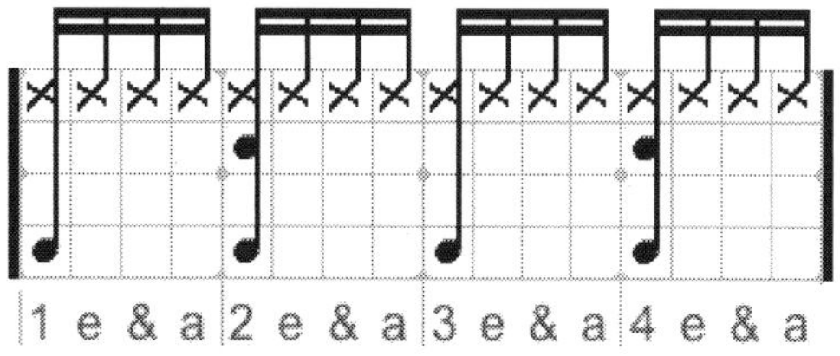

THE HIGH ROAD (BROKEN BELLS)

(2010) tempo = 80 bpm

SECTION NAME	PART TO PLAY	NOTES
Intro	— (x 4 measures)	
Vamp/verse	A (x 3)	
Chorus	B (x 2)	
Post-C/verse	A (x 4)	*break 3rd 'A'
Chorus	B (x 2)	
Post-C	A (x 1)	
Bridge	— (x 4 measures)	
	B (x 4)	*fade out

WHAT IT'S LIKE (EVERLAST)

(1998) tempo = 85 bpm

SECTION NAME	PART TO PLAY	NOTES
Intro	— (x 2)	
Verse 1	A (x 3)	
Chorus	B (x 2)	
Breakdown	— (x 1)	
Verse 2	A (x 4)	
Chorus	B (x 2)	
Break	— (x 1)	
Breakdown	A (x 2)	
Break	— (x 1)	
Verse 3	A (x 4)	
Chorus	B (x 1)	+2 measures
Outro	B (x 3)	

ONCE IN A WHILE (BREAK SCIENCE)

(2013) tempo = 85 bpm

SECTION NAME	PART TO PLAY	NOTES
Intro	A (x 2)	
Verse 1	A (x 2)	
Chorus	B (x 2)	*no drums last 2 measures
Vamp	B (x 1)	
Break	— (x 1)	
Verse 2	A (x 2)	*no drums last 2 measures
Vamp	A (x 2)	+2 BEATS
Chorus	B (x 2)	

6 UNDERGROUND (SNEAKER PIMPS)

(1996) tempo = 88 bpm

SECTION NAME	PART TO PLAY	NOTES
Intro	— (x 4 measures)	
Vamp/verse	A (x 3)	
Chorus	B (x 2)	
Break	— (x 4 measures)	
Vamp/verse	A (x 3)	
Chorus	B (x 2)	
Vamp	A (x 1)	
Chorus	B (x 2)	
Break	— (2 measures)	
Verse 3	A (x 2)	*no drums 1st two measures
Chorus	B (x 4)	+1 measure
Outro	A (x 1)	
Break	— (x 4 measures)	

*Feel free to substitute other grooves and fills.

SONG PART #2
(TEMPOS 90-110)

(INSTRUCTIONS, p.12)

SONG STRUCTURES >>

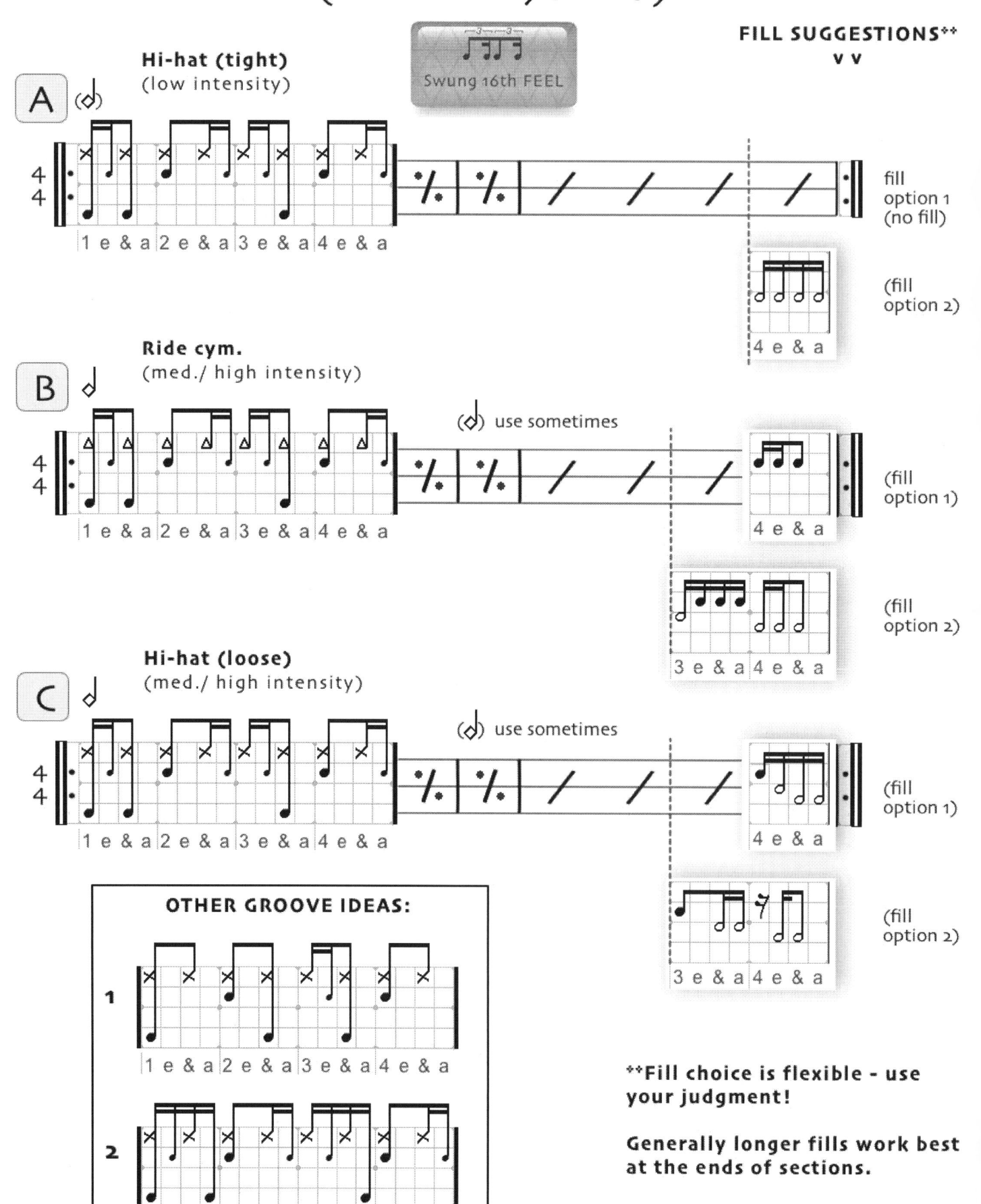

FILL SUGGESTIONS*
v v

Swung 16th FEEL

A Hi-hat (tight) (low intensity)

fill option 1 (no fill)

(fill option 2)

B Ride cym. (med./ high intensity)

(♩) use sometimes

(fill option 1)

(fill option 2)

C Hi-hat (loose) (med./ high intensity)

(♩) use sometimes

(fill option 1)

OTHER GROOVE IDEAS:

1

2

(fill option 2)

Fill choice is flexible - use your judgment!

Generally longer fills work best at the ends of sections.

32

WINDOWS (ANDERS OSBORNE)

(2013) tempo = 96 bpm

SECTION NAME	PART TO PLAY	NOTES
Vamp/verse	A (x 5)	
Chorus	B (x 1)	
Vamp/verse	A (x 5)	
Chorus	B (x 1)	
Vamp/verse	A (x 5)	
Chorus	B (x 1)	
Vamp	A (x 1)	
Sax solo	A (x 2)	
Chorus	B (x 1)	
Vamp	A (x 1)	
Gtr. solo	C (x 5)	
	B (x 1)	

STILL NOT DEAD (DREAMERS, AMERICAN TEETH, WES PERIOD)

(2021) tempo = 98 bpm

SECTION NAME	PART TO PLAY	NOTES
Vamp/verse	A (x 3)	
Chorus	B (x 2)	
Vamp/verse	A (x 4)	
Chorus	B (x 2)	
Vamp/verse	A (x 4)	
Break	— (x 11 measures)	
Chorus	B (x 3)	

MIAMI (FOALS)

(2010) tempo = 97 bpm

SECTION NAME	PART TO PLAY	NOTES
Vamp	A (x 1)	
	C (x 1)	
Verse 1	A (x 4)	
Chorus	B (x 2)	
Verse 2	A (x 3)	
Chorus	B (x 2)	
Vamp	A (x 2)	
	C (x 2)	
Chorus	B (x 4)	
Outro	— (x 4 measures)	

TOO MUCH (SOULIVE, NIGEL HALL)

(2009) tempo = 106 bpm

SECTION NAME	PART TO PLAY	NOTES
Vamp/verse	A (x 4)	
Pre-chorus	C (x 2)	
Chorus	B (x 2)	
Vamp/verse	A (x 4)	
Pre-chorus	C (x 2)	
Chorus	B (x 2)	
Bridge	C (x 4)	
Solos	A (x 4)	
	C (x 2)	
Chorus	B (x 2)	

THE 'FEEL' OF HOW YOU PLAY THE DRUMS

IS MORE IMPORTANT THAN WHAT YOU PLAY,

ESPECIALLY WHEN IT COMES TO SONGS.

SONG PARTS FOR DRUMS
SECTION II:
8th Triplet Feel

8th Triplet FEEL

- SLOW SONGS (60-100 BPM) - P.36

- MEDIUM SONGS (100-125 BPM) - P.38

- FAST SONGS (125-160 BPM) - P.40

- HALFTIME-FEEL SONGS - P.42

PLAY DRUMS NOW
THE ULTIMATE DRUMSET TRAINING PROGRAM

*Feel free to substitute other grooves and fills.

SONG PART #1
(TEMPOS 60-100)

(INSTRUCTIONS, p.12)

SONG STRUCTURES >>

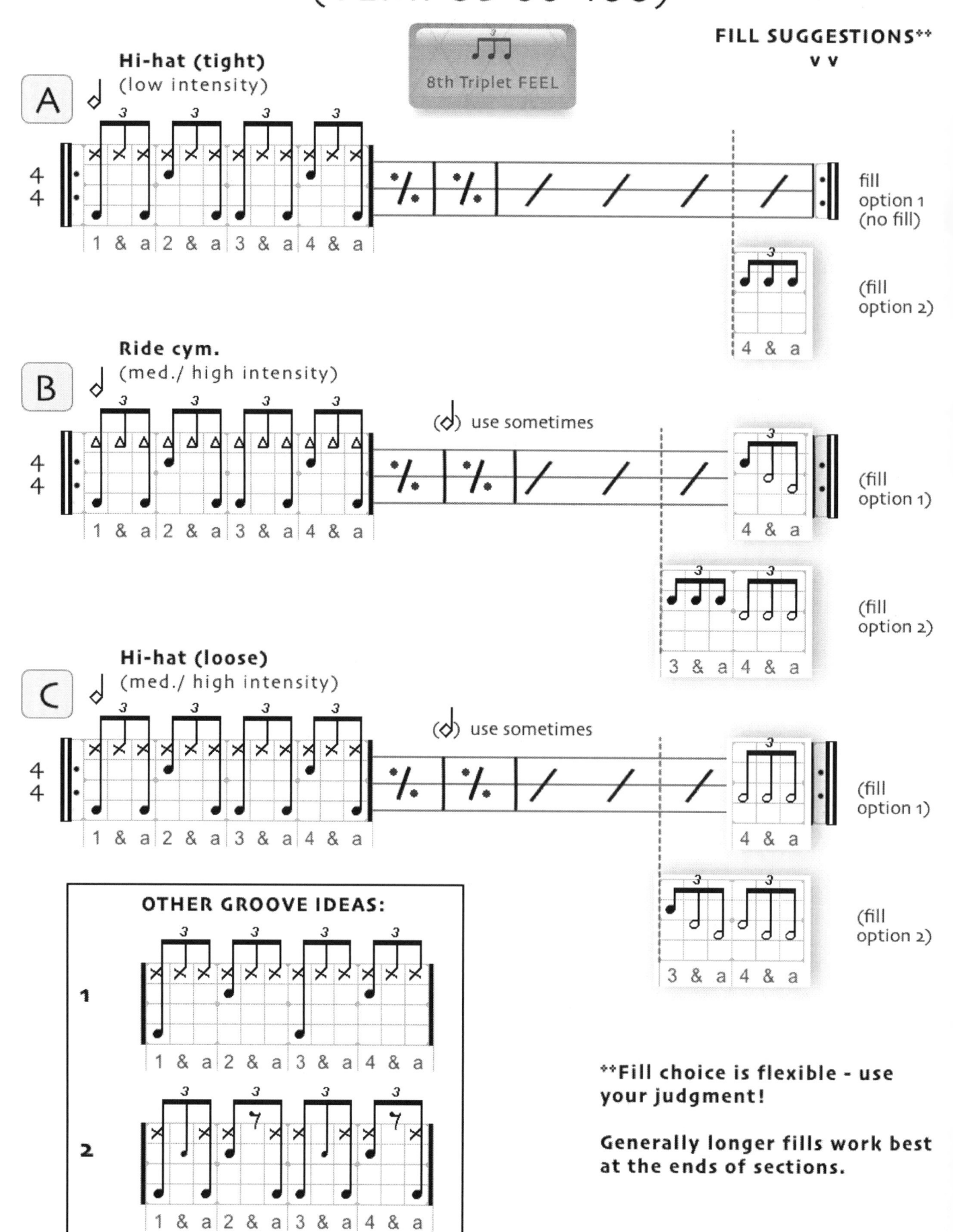

FILL SUGGESTIONS**
v v

8th Triplet FEEL

A — Hi-hat (tight) (low intensity)

fill option 1 (no fill)

(fill option 2)

B — Ride cym. (med./ high intensity)

(♩) use sometimes

(fill option 1)

(fill option 2)

C — Hi-hat (loose) (med./ high intensity)

(♩) use sometimes

(fill option 1)

(fill option 2)

OTHER GROOVE IDEAS:

1

2

****Fill choice is flexible - use your judgment!**

Generally longer fills work best at the ends of sections.

RED HOUSE (JIMI HENDRIX)

(1967) tempo = 66 bpm

SECTION NAME	PART TO PLAY	NOTES
Intro	— (x 4 measures)	*drum fill last measure
Gtr. solo	C (x 2)	
Verse 1	C (x 3)	
Verse 2	C (x 3)	
Gtr. solo	B (x 3)	
Verse 3	C (x 3)	*break 2nd measure of last group

LIGHTS (JOURNEY)

(1978) tempo = 68 bpm

SECTION NAME	PART TO PLAY	NOTES
Intro	— (x 4 measures)	
Chorus	A (x 2)	*break last measure
Verse 1	A (x 2)	
Bridge	B (x 2)	
Chorus	A (x 2)	
Gtr. solo	B (x 2)	
Chorus	B (x 2)	+1 measure

HOUSE OF BROKEN LOVE (GREAT WHITE)

(1989) tempo = 77 bpm

SECTION NAME	PART TO PLAY	NOTES
Vamp	A (x 1)	
Gtr. solo	A (x 3)	+2 measures
	B (x 3)	+2 measures
Verse 1	A (x 2)	
Chorus	B (x 3)	*break during 2nd 'B'
Verse 2	A (x 2)	
Chorus	B (x 2)	*break during 2nd 'B'
Bridge	B (x 1)	
Gtr. solo	C (x 2)	
Verse 3	A (x 2)	
Chorus	B (x 2)	*pause near end
Gtr. solo	B (x 4)	

BLACK VELVET (ALANNAH MILES)

(1989) tempo = 91 bpm

SECTION NAME	PART TO PLAY	NOTES
Vamp	A (x 2)	
Verse 1	A (x 3)	
Chorus	B (x 1)	+3 measures *break last measure
Vamp	A (x 1)	
Verse 2	A (x 3)	
Chorus	B (x 2)	+1 measure
Bridge	A (x 2)	*break last 2 measures
Gtr. solo	C (x 2)	
Chorus	B (x 3)	+2 measures
Break (pause)		
Outro	A (x 6)	*fade out

*Feel free to substitute other grooves and fills.

SONG PART #2
(TEMPOS 100-125)

(INSTRUCTIONS, p.12)

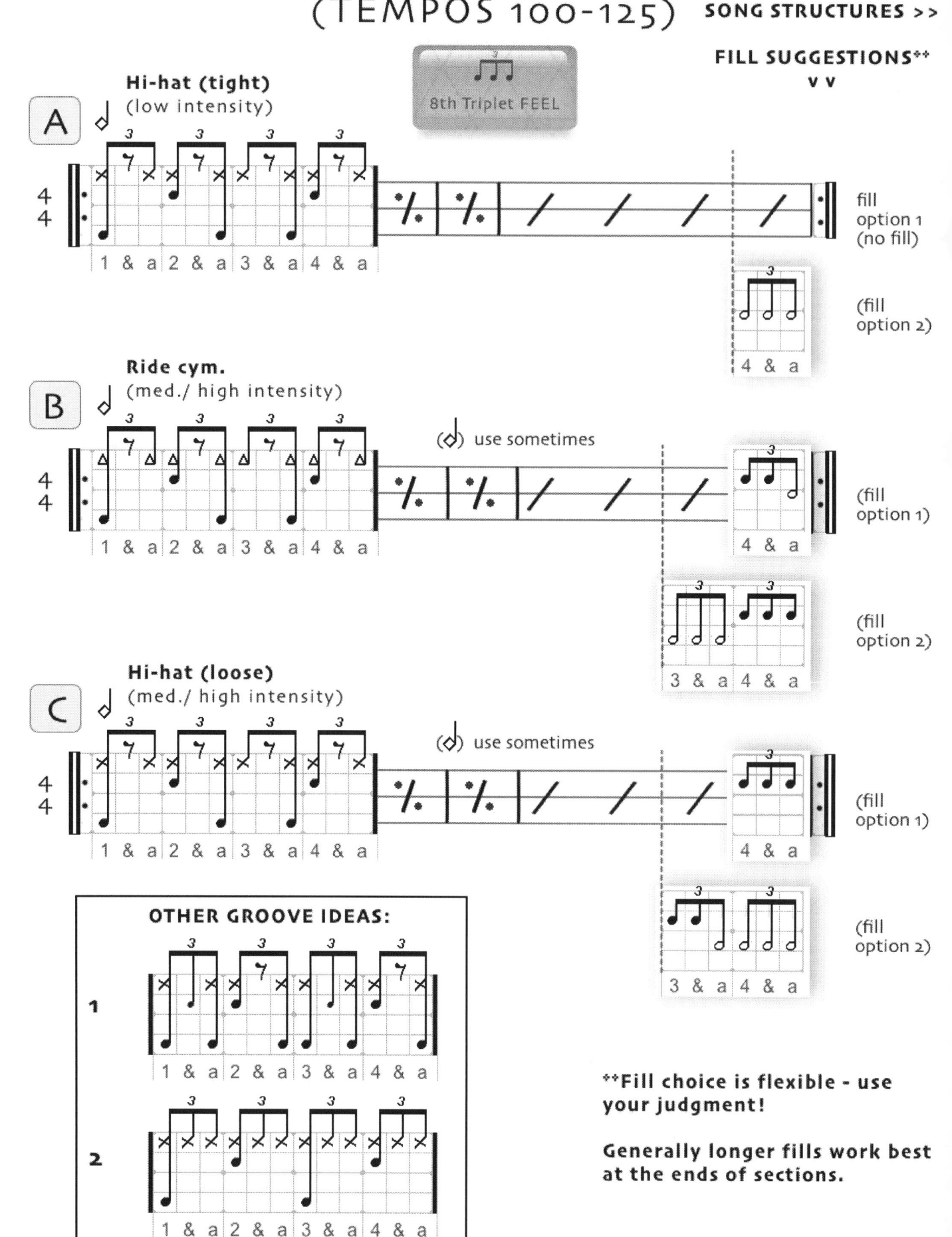

SONG STRUCTURES >>

FILL SUGGESTIONS*
v v

8th Triplet FEEL

A — Hi-hat (tight) (low intensity)

fill option 1 (no fill)

(fill option 2)

B — Ride cym. (med./ high intensity)

(♩) use sometimes

(fill option 1)

(fill option 2)

C — Hi-hat (loose) (med./ high intensity)

(♩) use sometimes

(fill option 1)

(fill option 2)

OTHER GROOVE IDEAS:

1

2

**Fill choice is flexible - use your judgment!

Generally longer fills work best at the ends of sections.

ALRIGHT
(ELECTRIC LIGHT ORCHESTRA)

(2001) tempo = 106 bpm

SECTION NAME	PART TO PLAY	NOTES
Vamp	A (x 1)	
Verse 1	A (x 2)	
Chorus	C (x 1)	+2 measures
Verse 2	A (x 2)	
Chorus	C (x 2)	+2 measures
Bridge	B (x 2)	+1/2 measure
Vamp	A (x 1)	
Verse 3	A (x 2)	
Chorus	C (x 2)	+2 measures
	C (x 3)	+3 measures

THE MOMENT (TAME IMPALA)

(2015) tempo = 119 bpm

SECTION NAME	PART TO PLAY	NOTES
Vamp	A (x 2)	
Verse 1	A (x 4)	
Chorus	A (x 2)	+1 measure
Verse 2	A (x 2)	
Chorus	A (x 2)	
Bridge	B (x 4)	
Break	— (x 12 measures)	
Vamp	A (x 2)	
Break	— (x 8 measures)	
Bridge	B (x 8)	

EITHER YOU WANT IT
(ROYAL BLOOD)

(2021) tempo = 117 bpm

SECTION NAME	PART TO PLAY	NOTES
Intro fill	(1 measure)	
Chorus vamp	C (x 2)	
Verse 1	A (x 3)	
Chorus	C (x 2)	
Verse 2	A (x 3)	
Chorus	C (x 3)	+2 measures
Bridge	B (x 3)	
Chorus	C (x 4)	

LEAVE ME ALONE
(MICHAEL JACKSON)

(1987) tempo = 124 bpm

SECTION NAME	PART TO PLAY	NOTES
Intro	— (x 4 measures)	*fill at end
Vamp	A (x 2)	
Verse 1	A (x 6)	*break last measure
Chorus	C (x 2)	
Vamp	A (x 1)	
Verse 2	A (x 6)	*break last measure
Chorus	C (x 2)	
Vamp	A (x 1)	
Bridge	B (x 3)	
Verse 3	A (x 2)	*break last measure
Chorus	C (x 4)	
Outro	A (x 4)	*fade out

*Feel free to substitute other grooves and fills.

SONG PART #3
(TEMPOS 125-160)

(INSTRUCTIONS, p.12)

SONG STRUCTURES >>

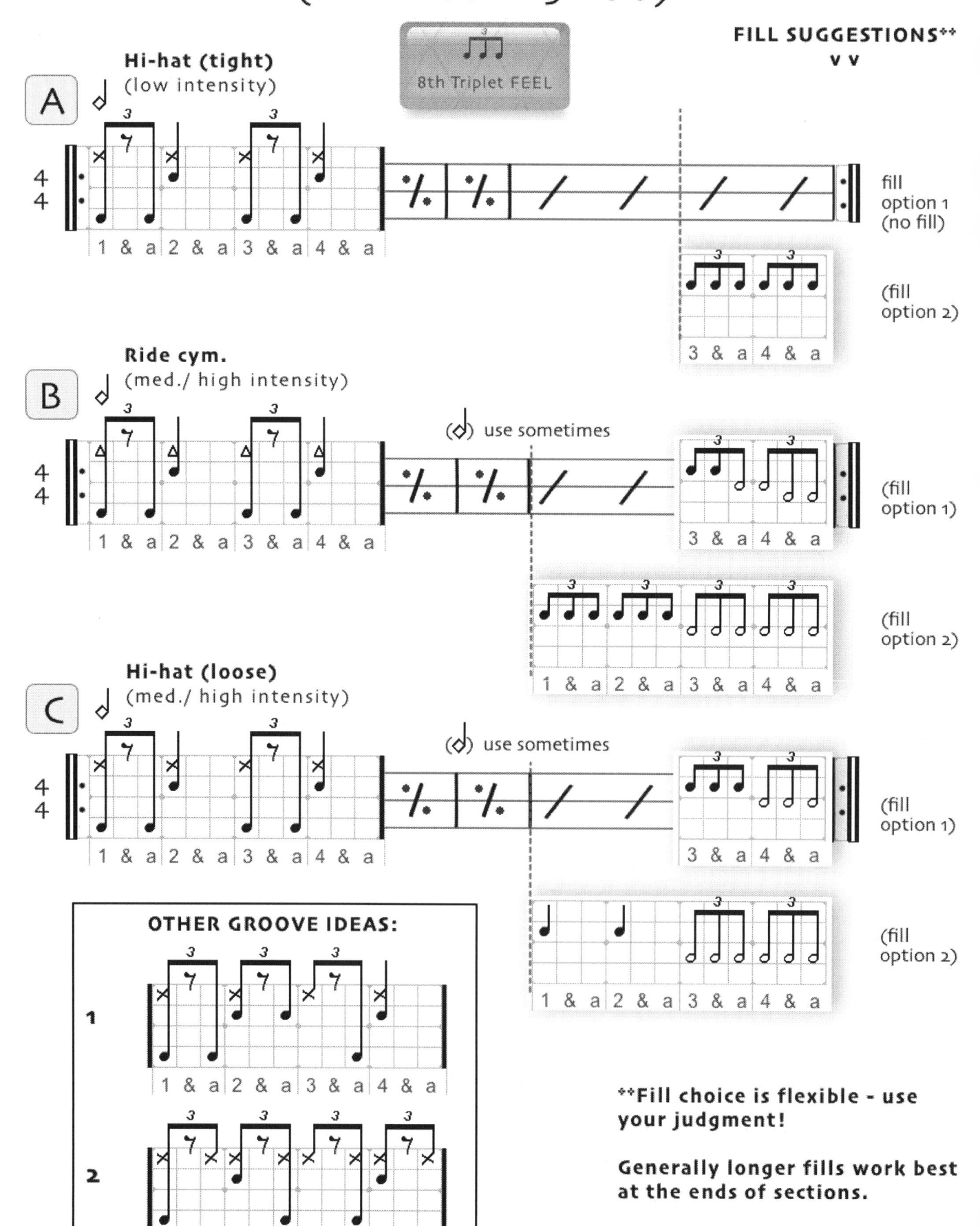

FILL SUGGESTIONS*
v v

8th Triplet FEEL

A — Hi-hat (tight) (low intensity)

fill option 1 (no fill)

(fill option 2)

B — Ride cym. (med./ high intensity)

(♩) use sometimes

(fill option 1)

(fill option 2)

C — Hi-hat (loose) (med./ high intensity)

(♩) use sometimes

(fill option 1)

(fill option 2)

OTHER GROOVE IDEAS:

1

2

**Fill choice is flexible - use your judgment!

Generally longer fills work best at the ends of sections.

40

STOCKHOLM (ATLAS GENIUS)

(2015) tempo = 125 bpm

SECTION NAME	PART TO PLAY	NOTES
Intro	— (x 8 measures)	
Vamp/verse	A (x 7)	
Chorus	B (x 4)	
Verse	A (x 4)	*break 1st 2 measures
Chorus	B (x 6)	
Outro	C (x 6 measures)	

HIGHER GROUND (RED HOT CHILI PEPPERS)

*original version by Stevie Wonder

(1989) tempo = 141 bpm

SECTION NAME	PART TO PLAY	NOTES
Intro	— (x 4 measures)	
Vamp	C (x 2)	
Verse 1	A (x 3)	
Vamp	C (x 1)	
Verse 2	A (x 3)	
Vamp	C (x 1)	
Chorus	B (x 2)	
Vamp	C (x 1)	
Verse 1	A (x 3)	
Vamp	C (x 1)	
Verse 2	A (x 3)	
Vamp	C (x 1)	
Chorus	B (x 2)	
Vamp	C (x 4)	
Outro	(faster, 4 measures)	

FAKE IT (SEETHER)

(2007) tempo = 132 bpm

SECTION NAME	PART TO PLAY	NOTES
Verse 1	— (x 8 measures)	*groove starts last measure
Pre-C/chorus	C (x 4)	
Verse 2	A (x 2)	
Pre-C/chorus	C (x 4)	
Bridge 1	B (x 2)	
Gtr. solo	A (x 2)	
Bridge 2	C (x 2)	
Verse 3	— (x 8 measures)	*groove starts last measure
Pre-C/chorus	C (x 6)	

ELECTIONEERING (RADIOHEAD)

(1997) tempo = 157 bpm

SECTION NAME	PART TO PLAY	NOTES
Intro	— (x 4 measures)	
Vamp	C (x 2)	
Verse	C (x 5)	
Chorus	B (x 4)	
Vamp	C (x 2)	
Verse	C (x 5)	
Chorus	B (x 4)	
Break (pause)		
Guitar solo	C (x 8)	

*Feel free to substitute other grooves and fills.

SONG PART #4 (HALFTIME FEEL)

(INSTRUCTIONS, p.12)

SONG STRUCTURES >>

FILL SUGGESTIONS**
v v

Hi-hat (tight)
(low intensity)

A

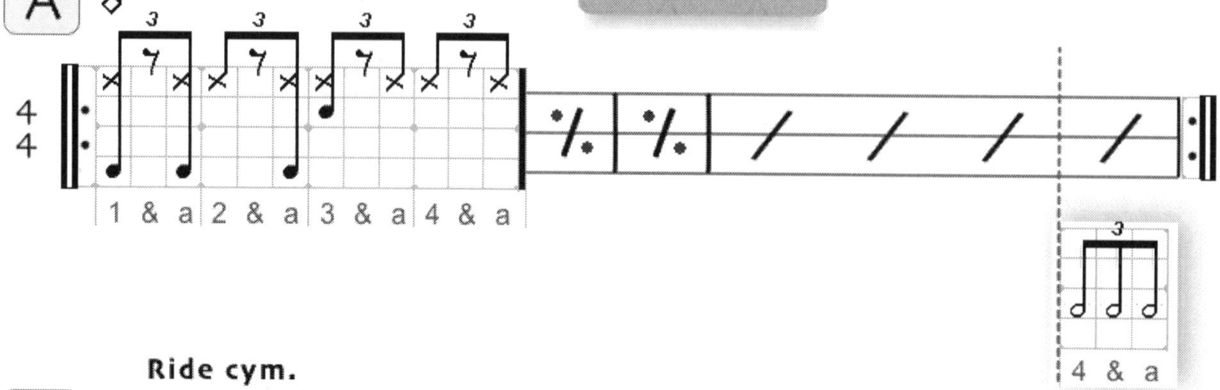

fill option 1 (no fill)

(fill option 2)

Ride cym.
(med./ high intensity)

B

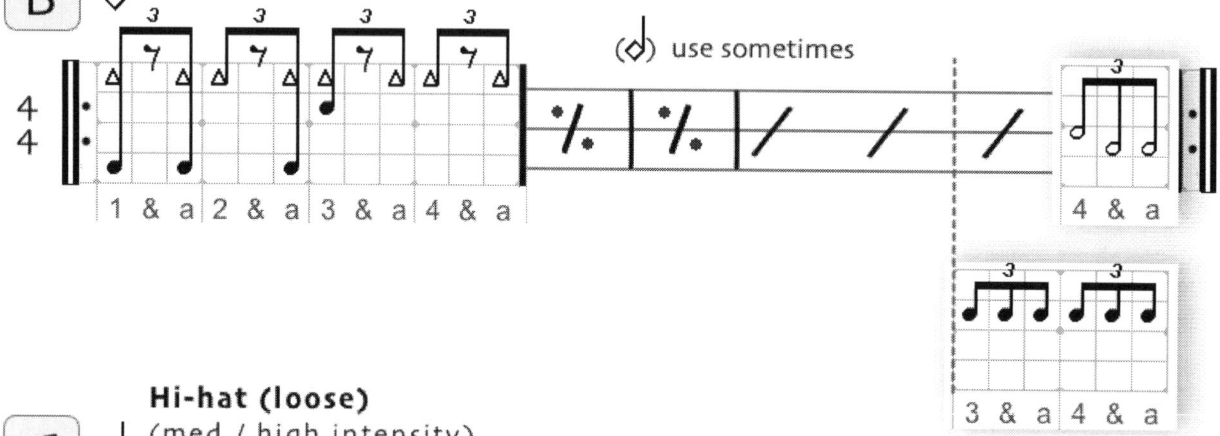

(fill option 1)

(fill option 2)

Hi-hat (loose)
(med./ high intensity)

C

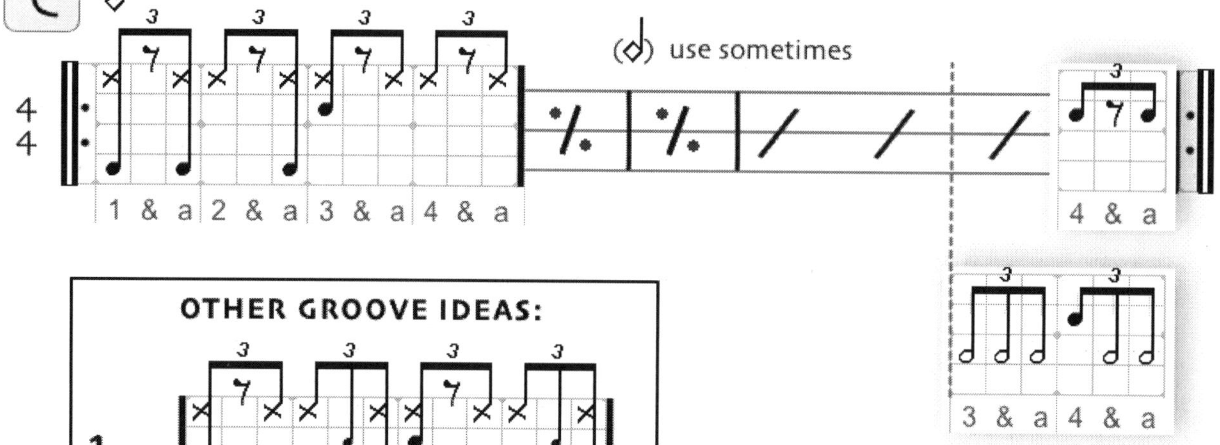

(fill option 1)

(fill option 2)

OTHER GROOVE IDEAS:

1

2

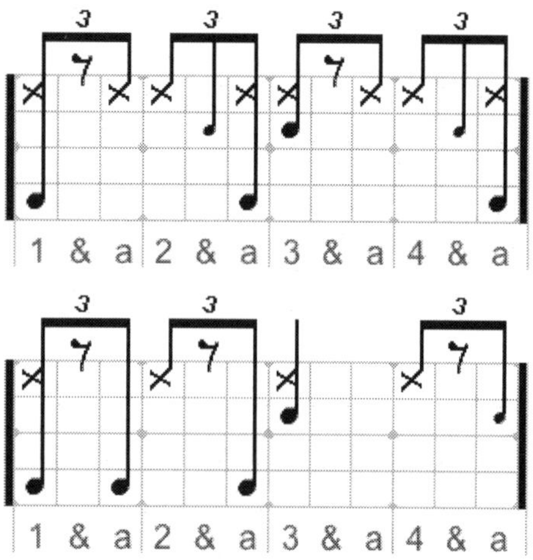

****Fill choice is flexible - use your judgment!**

Generally longer fills work best at the ends of sections.

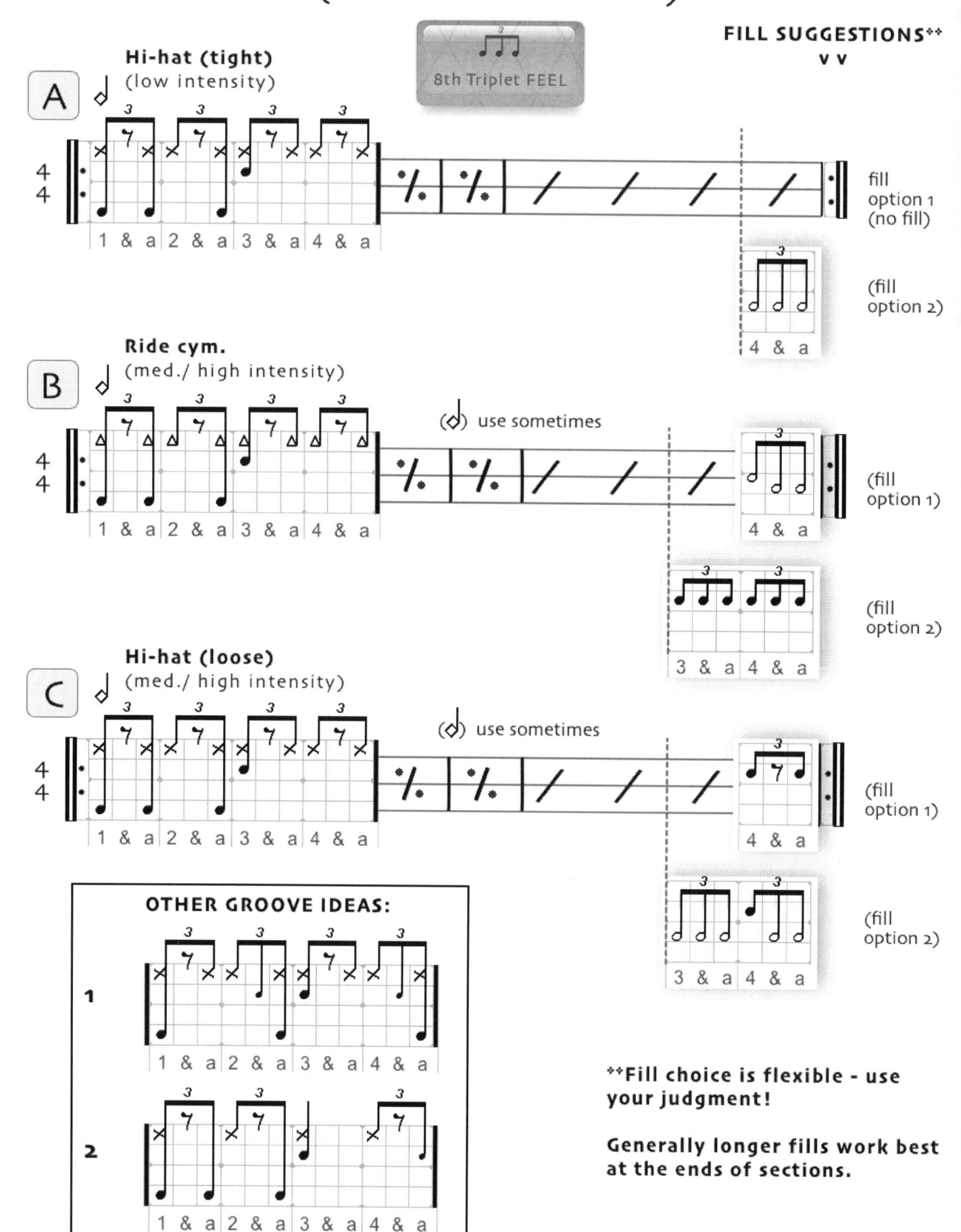

BELIEVER (IMAGINE DRAGONS, LIL WAYNE)

(2019) tempo = 125 bpm

SECTION NAME	PART TO PLAY	NOTES
Vamp	A (x 1)	
Verse 1	A (x 6)	
Chorus	C (x 4)	
Verse 2	A (x 6)	
Chorus	C (x 4)	
Verse 3	A (x 3)	
Chorus	C (x 4)	

SAVE YOURSELF (BREAKING BENJAMIN)

(2018) tempo = 133 bpm

SECTION NAME	PART TO PLAY	NOTES
Vamp	C (x 2)	
Verse 1	A (x 2)	
	C (x 2)	
Break	— (x 2 measures)	
Chorus	B (x 3)	+2 measures
Vamp	C (x 2)	
Verse 2	A (x 2)	
	C (x 2)	
Break	— (x 2 measures)	
Chorus	B (x 3)	+2 measures
Vamp	C (x 2)	
Chorus	B (x 3)	+2 measures
Vamp	C (x 1)	

SKY IS A NEIGHBORHOOD (FOO FIGHTERS)

(2017) tempo = 133 bpm

SECTION NAME	PART TO PLAY	NOTES
Intro	— (x 8 measures)	
Chorus	A (x 4)	
	B (x 6)	
Verse 1	A (x 4)	
Chorus	B (x 6)	
Bridge	C (x 1)	+2 measures
Break	— (x 9 measures)	*fill at end
Chorus	B (x 6)	
Bridge	C (x 1)	+2 measures

BETTER STRANGERS (ROYAL BLOOD)

(2014) tempo = 141 bpm

SECTION NAME	PART TO PLAY	NOTES
Vamp/verse	A (x 4)	+2 measures
Vamp/verse	A (x 3)	+2 measures
Chorus	C (x 3)	+2 measures
Vamp/verse	A (x 3)	+2 measures
Chorus	C (x 4)	
Bridge	C (x 3)	
Vamp/verse	A (x 4)	+2 measures
Chorus	C (x 7)	+2 measures

A KNIFE IN THE OCEAN (FOALS)

(2015) tempo = 119 bpm

SECTION NAME	PART TO PLAY	NOTES
Intro	— (x 16 measures)	
Vamp	A (x 2)	
Verse 1	A (x 4)	
Vamp	A (x 2)	
Chorus	B (x 4)	
Vamp	A (x 2)	
Verse 2	A (x 4)	
Chorus	B (x 4)	
Break	— (x 12 measures)	
Vamp	A (x 4)	
Chorus	B (x 8)	
Outro	B (x 4)	

GRAPEVINE FIRES (DEATH CAB FOR CUTIE)

(2008) tempo = 124 bpm

SECTION NAME	PART TO PLAY	NOTES
Vamp	A (x 1)	
Verse 1	A (x 4)	
Chorus	C (x 4)	
Verse 2	A (x 4)	
Chorus	C (x 4)	
Bridge	— (x 16 measures)	
Chorus	C (x 4)	
	B (x 4)	
Outro	— (x 6 measures)	

THE FLOCK (DAVID MAXIM MICIC, SCAMPI)

(2015) tempo = 140 bpm

SECTION NAME	PART TO PLAY	NOTES
Intro	— (x 16 measures)	
Vamp/verse	A (x 12)	
Chorus	B (x 4)	
Break	— (x 8 measures)	
Verse 2	A (x 4)	
Chorus	B (x 4)	
Bridge 1	C (x 4)	
Break	— (x 20 measures)	
Bridge 2	B (x 3)	
Break	— (x 12 measures)	
Chorus	— (x 16 measures)	
(Chorus)	B (x 8)	

ANOTHER WORLD (GOJIRA)

(2021) tempo = 180 bpm

SECTION NAME	PART TO PLAY	NOTES
Vamp	C (x 4)	
Verse 1	B (x 4)	
Chorus	C (x 4)	
Verse 2	B (x 4)	
Chorus	C (x 4)	
Bridge	C (x 12)	
Chorus	C (x 4)	
Outro	— (x 16 measures)	

SONG PARTS FOR DRUMS

SECTION III:

6/8 Time Feel

6/8 Time FEEL

- ALL SONGS (150-200 BPM) - P.46

PLAY DRUMS NOW
THE ULTIMATE DRUMSET TRAINING PROGRAM

*Feel free to substitute other grooves and fills.

SONG PART #1
(TEMPOS 150-200)

(INSTRUCTIONS, p.12)

SONG STRUCTURES >>

FILL SUGGESTIONS*
v v

6/8 Time FEEL

A — Hi-hat (tight) (low intensity)

fill option 1 (no fill)

(fill option 2)

B — Ride cym. (med./ high intensity)

(♩) use sometimes

(fill option 1)

(fill option 2)

C — Hi-hat (loose) (med./ high intensity)

(♩) use sometimes

(fill option 1)

(fill option 2)

OTHER GROOVE IDEAS:

1

2

**Fill choice is flexible - use your judgment!

Generally longer fills work best at the ends of sections.

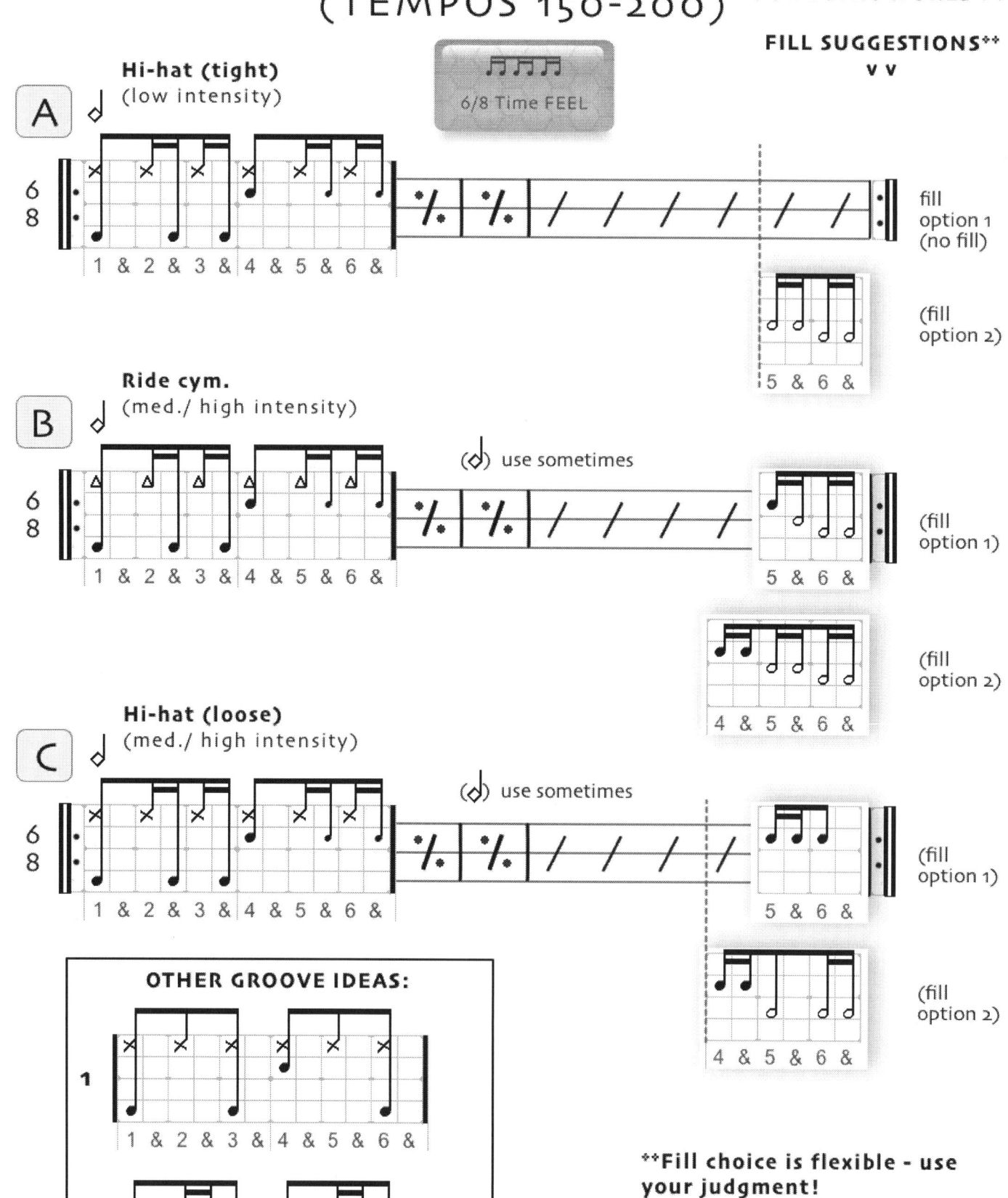

46

DANCE WITH THE DEVIL (BREAKING BENJAMIN)

(2006) tempo = 155 bpm

SECTION NAME	PART TO PLAY	NOTES
Intro	— (x 4 measures)	
Vamp	C (x 1)	
Verse 1	A (x 2)	*play groove on toms
Pre-chorus	C (x 2)	
Chorus	B (x 2)	+2 measures
Verse 2	A (x 2)	
Pre-chorus	C (x 2)	
Chorus	B (x 2)	
Bridge	C (x 3)	
Chorus	B (x 2)	
Bridge	C (x 1)	
Outro	A (x 1)	+2 measures *play groove on toms

SUBTERRANEAN HOMESICK ALIEN (RADIOHEAD)

(1997) tempo = 152 bpm

SECTION NAME	PART TO PLAY	NOTES
Intro	— (x 4 measures)	
Vamp	B (x 2)	
Verse 1	A (x 2)	
Vamp	B (x 1)	
Verse 2	A (x 1)	
Chorus	C (x 2)	+2 measures
Vamp	B (x 2)	
Verse 3	A (x 1)	+2 measures
Break (pause)		
Vamp	B (x 2)	
Chorus	C (x 3)	+2 measures
Vamp	B (x 2)	

PINK AND WHITE (FRANK OCEAN)

(2016) tempo = 160 bpm

SECTION NAME	PART TO PLAY	NOTES
Vamp	A (x 1)	
Verse 1	B (x 7)	
Verse 2	A (x 5)	
Verse 3	B (x 6)	

WALK ON THE OCEAN (TOAD THE WET SPROCKET)

(1991) tempo = 183 bpm

SECTION NAME	PART TO PLAY	NOTES
Verse 1	A (x 4)	
Chorus	B (x 4)	
Verse 2	A (x 4)	
Chorus	B (x 4)	
Solo	B (x 4)	
Verse 3	C (x 2)	*no drums last 2 measures
	A (x 1)	+2 measures

JUDITH (A PERFECT CIRCLE)

(2000) tempo = 165 bpm

SECTION NAME	PART TO PLAY	NOTES
Vamp	C (x 3)	
Verse 1	A (x 2)	
Pre-chorus	C (x 2)	
Chorus	C (x 2)	
Post-chorus	B (x 3)	+2 measures
Break	— (x 4 measures)	
Verse 2	A (x 3)	
Chorus	C (x 2)	
Post-chorus	B (x 5)	+2 measures
Outro	C (x 2)	

MOTHERS DREAM (CANDLEBOX)

(1993) tempo = 196 bpm

SECTION NAME	PART TO PLAY	NOTES
Vamp	B (x 4)	
Verse 1	A (x 4)	
Vamp	B (x 2)	
Verse 2	A (x 4)	
Chorus	C (x 4)	
Vamp/solo	B (x 4)	
Verse 3	A (x 4)	
Chorus	C (x 3)	
Vamp	B (x 5)	*fade out

THE KILL (30 SECONDS TO MARS)

(2005) tempo = 183 bpm

SECTION NAME	PART TO PLAY	NOTES
Verse 1	A (x 4)	
Chorus	C (x 2)	
Verse 2	A (x 4)	
Chorus	C (x 4)	
Bridge	B (x 4)	
Break	— (x 10 measures)	*play fills
Chorus	C (x 6)	
Verse 3	A (x 2)	

FLOATY (FOO FIGHTERS)

(1995) tempo = 228 bpm

SECTION NAME	PART TO PLAY	NOTES
Intro	— (16 measures)	
Verse 1	A (x 4)	+2 measures
Verse 2	A (x 4)	+2 measures
Chorus	C (x 4)	
Verse 3	A (x 4)	+2 measures
Chorus	C (x 4)	
Bridge	B (x 3)	+4.5 measures
Verse 4	A (x 4)	+2 measures
Bridge	B (x 3)	+2 measures
Bridge	B (x 3)	+2 measures

Did you complete this book?

CONGRATS!!!

NICE WORK.

SKILLS ASSESSMENT:

Check these criteria to see if you're ready to move on from this book!

- You understand the knowledge and wisdom in the written sections of this book
- You have experienced an increase in skill from training with this material
- You can play any of the exercises in this book at a comfortable tempo
- You feel confident in your ability to learn and play new similar material
- You are motivated to learn more and become a better drummer

NEXT STEPS:

- **Continue on to the LEVEL 3 MATERIALS!!** You are now at an ADVANCED status of training.
- Go to www.PlayDrumsNow.com for more resources.

ABOUT THE AUTHOR:

Adam Randall - Drummer, educator, and author. Adam has performed and recorded drums professionally with bands across various styles. His career in drum instruction started with ten years at the Colorado Music Institute, and he has since been teaching at Klash Drums in MN. He published his first books on drum instruction in 2010, and he continues to create new materials as part of his mission to make it easier for people to become great drummers.

Follow @playdrumsnow on Instagram, facebook, twitter, youtube etc. for more!

WWW.PLAYDRUMSNOW.COM
ADAM RANDALL

GENERAL PRACTICE TIPS

PRACTICING IS IMPORTANT because your body has a **physical memory,** which is very different from (and learns a bit slower than) your cognitive memory. YOU MUST BE PATIENT while teaching yourself any physical pattern you want to play on the drums!

> "The more times in a row you do something the same way, the more your body can remember the action without your conscious mind."

Make sure to keep your 'PLAYING' and 'PRACTICING' separate, and spend time each week doing both. 'Playing' is good for having fun, but 'practicing' is what creates progress.

'PLAYING' is when you allow your drumming to be fun and expressive, maybe spontaneous and creative. It's when you are using drumming as a musical art form, or just simply enjoying doing stuff you already know how to do.

'PRACTICING' is when you repeat some unfamiliar action carefully, until it becomes easier and more familiar and you GAIN CONTROL. Also known as 'rehearsing'.

THE 'IDEAL PRACTICE METHOD'
for learning any pattern

1. Read and imagine the exercise.

Imagine what your body is about to do

2. Play one count at a time, slowly and in control - no mistakes!

At least four consecutive measures

3. Play / loop the exercise with correct timing / rhythm.

Keep tempo steady, and look away from the written music.

4. Explore various tempos.

Try playing faster than you think you can handle, you'll often be surprised!

5. Improve the pattern's quality and your physical actions to play it.

Listen to the exercise as you play it, and observe how it feels physically to play it.

HOW OFTEN TO PRACTICE?

CASUAL: 30 - 60 min per week

SERIOUS: 1-2 hours per week

PRO: 3+ hours per week

Printed in France by Amazon
Brétigny-sur-Orge, FR